City Dog

The National Hotel & Resort Guide

For You and Your Dog

ISBN 1-933068-00-0

Editor: Cricky Long
Content Manager: Bryce Longton
Production Coordinator: Jamie Wetherbe
Cover Illustration: Bill Kheel
Cover Design: Jennifer L. Ciminillo
Copy Editor: David Skaugerud
Hotel Editor: Bryce Longton
Hotel Writers: Faisal Adams   Nancy Ball
　　　　　　　　Kate Beale   Michelle Burton
　　　　　　　　Laurie Turner   Stephanie Diaz
　　　　　　　　Tamar Love   Coco McPherson
　　　　　　　　Darryl Morden   Vanessa Nichols
　　　　　　　　Bill Retherford   Heather Shouse

City Dog
P.O. Box 69216
West Hollywood, CA 90069
(323) 857-5217 (phone)
(323) 857-5216 (fax)
www.citydog.net

The purpose of the guidebook is to inform and to entertain. Every effort was made to ensure that all information contained in this guidebook was accurate and up-to-date at the time of publication. However, the authors, editor and City Dog Publishing, LLC shall have neither liability nor responsibility to any person or entity with respect to any loss or damage caused, or alleged to have been caused, directly or indirectly, by the information contained in this book. It is recommended that you call ahead to confirm business information.

Acknowledgments

This book would not have been possible without the tireless efforts of everyone involved, especially Bryce, Elizabeth, Eric, Hal, Jamie, Nehme and Scott. Gus, Robert, Betty and Henry also deserve special thanks for all of their advice and support.

Table of Contents

Introduction 6

Legend 9

Arizona 10

Northern California 14

Southern California 31

Colorado 52

Connecticut 58

Delaware 60

Washington, D.C. 61

Florida 72

Georgia 84

Illinois 90

Indiana 97

Louisiana 98

Maine 102

Maryland 103

Massachusetts 104

Michigan 113

Minnesota 116

Missouri 118

Nevada 120

New Jersey 123

New Mexico 124

New York City 125

New York 142

North Carolina 145

Ohio 147

Oklahoma 150

Oregon 151

Pennsylvania 155

Rhode Island 160

South Carolina 161

Texas 163

Utah 174

Vermont 175

Virginia 177

Washington 180

Wyoming 185

In A Pinch Hotel Chain 186

Preparing & Packing 188

Airline Rules 191

Alphabetical Index 196

Introduction

Think of what a place this world could be if only we would all be the people our dogs think we are.

When we set about creating the first *City Dog* guidebook our mission was simple: Make people's lives easier so they can make their dogs' lives better. To that end, we researched every possible dog-care offering. The idea was that we would provide people with the names, phone numbers and reviews of dog-care providers. This would empower people to find someone reliable to jump in and take over dog detail when they discovered they were going to be stuck at work, or were suddenly called out of town.

In our travels, we compiled reviews on all of the hard-to-find resources, such as animal-behavior specialists; holistic vets; acupuncturists; chiropractors; massage therapists; and animal nutritionists. We also compiled a list of all the 24-hour and after-hours animal emergency facilities. We checked out all of the pet-supply stores, from the bargain shops to the high-end accessory boutiques. But we still had more useful dog-centric information than we knew what to do with, so we created appendixes: The Puppy Starter Kit, Lost Dog Help and When Dogs Go to Heaven.

We put it all together, and the result was *City Dog: The A-to-Z Guidebook of Dog Services and Shops.*

So basically, whatever you do, however quickly your plans change—*City Dog* has you covered. No matter where you are traveling to, you can rest assured that your dog is in the hands of a dog-care professional. Gone are the days of having to rely on the good will of your neighbor.

But what about when you want to take your dog with you?

Once people get over the initial excitement of having all of *City Dog's* city-specific resources at their fingertips, they immediately ask about dog-friendly hotels. It seems that the only thing better than knowing your dog is being properly cared for in your absence, is being able to take your dog with you.

It used to be that bringing your dog along on a trip meant sneaking them in and out of the hotel through a side door. These days, not only are dogs welcome in a number of U.S. hotels, but they are also treated to special perks, amenities and packages. In fact, we know of one lavish five-star hotel that will not accommodate children under 18 years old, yet dogs get free run of the grounds, plus a bed and freshly cooked meals.

And so, we were inspired to create *City Dog: The National Hotel & Resort Guide For You and Your Dog*. All of our favorite dog-friendly hotels in all the major cities—and a few small-town resorts—are listed and reviewed in this guidebook. In addition to informing you of hotel policies regarding weight limits and pet surcharges, we also cover all the pet perks, amenities and services each hotel offers. And you will find information on all of the people perks and quirks of each hotel. Additionally, the appendixes feature travel tips, packing lists and airline and car rental rules.

Happy trails!

How to Use This Guide

City Dog: The National Hotel & Resort Guide For You and Your Dog answers all of your "But what about my dog?" travel questions. This guidebook, which has been broken down by state and then by area code, contains the following information:

- The A-to-Z Directory of dog-friendly hotels in all major U.S. cities
- Hotel fees, policies and weight limits for your pup
- Essential information on airline and car rental rules
- Packing lists for your pup with location- and season-specific information
- User-friendly indexes

Legend

For those of you who don't like to read the fine print, we have created icons to make it easy for you to see at a glance which hotel suits you best.

Golfing
Facilities

Skiing
Facilities

Swimming Pool
Available

Business
Facilities

Family
Friendly

Spa

Gym

Dog Amenities

Romantic
Destination

Tourist
Hotel

Shopping

Hiking

Beach

Tennis Facilities

High-Speed
Internet

$ = Economy
$$$ = Moderate
$$$$ = Pricey
$$$$$ = Outragous

Arizona

(480) - Scottsdale

Four Seasons Resort: Scottsdale - Troon North
James Hotels Scottsdale
The Phoenician
The Westin: Kierland Resort & Spa

(520) - Tucson

The Westin: La Paloma Resort & Spa

(623) - Litchfield Park

The Wigwam Resort and Golf Club

(480) - Scottsdale

Four Seasons Resort: Scottsdale - Troon North

(480) 515-5700
10600 E Crescent Moon Dr
(off N Alma School Pkwy)
Scottsdale, Arizona 85262
www.fourseasons.com/scottsdale
Price Range: $$$$$

Relaxation seekers may simply want to sit by the pool and take in the stunning Southwest landscape or get a treatment at the spa. Golfers can check out Troon North, while tennis players will appreciate the courts—complete with night lights. For those who want to get off the beaten path, hiking, rock climbing and mountain biking are also on the itinerary. There's plenty here for dogs too: treats, bones and lots of hiking up nearby Pinnacle Peak. Keep in mind that the resort does not allow dogs to stay in the room unattended, so either keep your dog with you or be prepared to pay $20 per half-hour for dog-sitting. No fee. 15-pound weight limit.

James Hotel: Scottsdale

(888) 500-8080
7353 E Indian School Rd
(@ Drinkwater Blvd)
Scottsdale, California 85251
www.jameshotel.com/scottsdale

Price Range: $$$

Sexy, accommodating, a bit daring and very reasonably priced, the James has created an NC-17 playground for vacationers. Rooms include plasma TVs, wireless Internet, Lather bath products and plush beds. The 115-foot PLAYpool, complete with a bar, is just outside the gym, which is modeled after the Equinox Fitness Club in New York. Trainers, weights and yoga classes are standard offerings. Book ahead for their lavish spa services, which include a Paint By Number treatment and the Blend massage. All spa services are performed in Treatment Cabanas that have fireplaces and relaxing music. Fiamma serves delicious Italian fare. No specific weight limit: All small dogs welcome; larger dogs accepted on a case-by-case basis. $75 fee.

The Phoenician

(800) 888-8234
6000 E Camelback Rd
(@ N Phoenician Rd)
Scottsdale, Arizona 85251
www.thephoenician.com

Price Range: $$$$$

Everything you need for your stay is available on-site at this heavenly desert resort. The list includes heated pools, tennis and golf pros to help you with your game, a full-service spa that's a favorite of *Condé Nast Traveler* readers, as well as hair and nail salons. Children's offerings include an outdoor pool, playground, waterslide and supervised activities. Guests with dogs are relegated to the Casita section, conveniently located next to the lawn. The concierge and room service will make every effort to accommodate your canine, but you're the bottom line when it comes to your dog's dining and sleeping arrangements. $50 fee. 30-pound weight limit.

The Westin: Kierland Resort & Spa

(480) 624-1000
6902 E Greenway Pkwy
(@ Scottsdale Rd)
Scottsdale, Arizona 85254
www.kierlandresort.com
Price Range: $$$$

Adjacent to the shopping and restaurant mecca, Kierland Commons, this Westin offers spa facilities and treatments based on the healing traditions of old Arizona. The Westin restaurant, Deseo, features a Latin American menu. In the summertime, you will definitely appreciate the waterslide and two outdoor pools, one for adults and another for kids. The hotel takes care of its dog guests too, offering the Westin's signature Heavenly Dog Bed and an entire floor of pet-friendly rooms. A common walking area is steps away and always available for romping or dog socializing. No fee. No weight limit.

(520) – Tucson

The Westin: La Paloma Resort & Spa

(520) 742-6000
3800 E Sunrise Dr
(@ Via Palomita)
Tucson, Arizona 85718
www.westinlapalomaresort.com
Price Range: $$$$

This Westin, located at the foothills of the Santa Catalina Mountains, offers grand views of its 10,000-foot peaks. For a better vantage point, you can hike with your dog through Sabino Canyon inside Coronado National Forest. Possible sans-dog activities include a round of golf on the Jack

Nicklaus signature course, a game on one of 10 tennis courts, a swim in one of the three pools or a slide down the largest resort waterslide in Arizona. The hotel restaurant, Janos, serves up Southwestern cuisine. Dog offerings include the signature Westin Heavenly Dog Bed, nearby grassy walking areas and bags and gloves for pickup duties. No fee. 40-pound weight limit.

(623) - Litchfield Park

The Wigwam Resort and Golf Club
(800) 327-0396
300 E Wigwam Blvd
(off Sahuaro Rd)
Litchfield Park, Arizona 85340
www.wigwamresort.com
Price Range: $$$
This rustic, legendary Arizona landmark with adobe-style casitas and Native American design is a real people-pleaser. Kids can partake in a slue of outdoor activities at the resort's Camp Pow Wow. And your pup will love the acres of grass and lush flower gardens that will inspire frequent dog walks. If you feel like venturing out, a beautiful lake two blocks away is another dog-walking hot spot. A $50 deposit (half of which is refundable) and maximum weight of 30 pounds gains your pup entry into this resort, but amenities are on you.

Northern California

(415) – San Francisco

Argonaut Hotel
Four Seasons Hotel: San Francisco
Galleria Park Hotel
Harbor Court Hotel
Hotel Cosmo
Hotel Monaco: San Francisco
Hotel Palomar
Hotel Triton
Mandarin Oriental: San Francisco
Monticello Inn
Palace Hotel
The Prescott Hotel
The Ritz-Carlton: San Francisco
Serrano Hotel
The Sir Francis Drake
Tuscan Inn at Fisherman's Wharf
Villa Florence
W: San Francisco
The Westin: St. Francis

(707) – Calistoga, Healdsburg & Yountville

Calistoga Ranch
Hotel Healdsburg
Vintage Inn

(510) – Newark

W: Silicon Valley- Newark

(650) – Half Moon Bay, Palo Alto & Redwood City

The Ritz-Carlton: Half Moon Bay
The Westin: San Francisco Airport
The Westin: Palo Alto
Sofitel: San Francisco Bay

(408) – Cupertino

Cypress Hotel

(415) - San Francisco

Argonaut Hotel
(866) 415-0704
495 Jefferson St
(@ Hyde St)
San Francisco, California 94109
www.argonauthotel.com
Price Range: $$$
The nautical theme of this four-star Fisherman's Wharf bou-
tique hotel is brought to life by such quirky Kimpton-hotel
touches as oceanliner lounge chairs in the living room, as well
as guest rooms with exposed brick walls and steel doors. Perks
include room service from the Blue Mermaid Chowder House
and Bar, complimentary wine hour, business and fitness cen-
ters, plus special rooms with longer beds and higher shower-
heads for taller guests. The Argonaut allows only small- and
medium-sized dogs, and asks that you be reachable if you
leave your dog unattended in the room. You can also arrange
for a pet-sitter through the concierge. No fee.

Four Seasons Hotel: San Francisco
(415) 633-3000
757 Market St
(between 3rd & 4th sts)
San Francisco, California 94103
www.fourseasons.com/sanfrancisco
Price Range: $$$$$
This plush, romantic Four Seasons—boasting the largest rooms
in San Francisco, with floor-to-ceiling windows—has every-
thing a traveler might want. The financial district, the Moscone
Convention Center and Union Square are only blocks away, as
is Yerba Buena Gardens—a great place to take your pup for a
walk. Amenities include a Junior Olympic-sized pool, a
100,000-square-foot gym that offers spinning and weight train-
ing, and a full-service spa. You can also check out the

decadent Seasons Restaurant, which features an award-winning sushi bar. Dogs are not allowed to be left alone in the room but the hotel offers dog-walking and pet-sitting services. No fee. 15-pound weight limit.

Galleria Park Hotel
(866) 756-3036
191 Sutter St
(@ Kearny St)
San Francisco, California 94104
www.galleriapark.com
Price Range: $$$

This swanky, nouveau-style Kimpton hotel is near the sights and shopping of Union Square, as well as the financial district. MOMA and the Moscone Convention Center are also within walking distance. Hotel perks include a rooftop park with a jogging track, a nightly wine hour and a 24-hour business center. The Tek Talk package—perfect for the business traveler— includes wireless Internet and Starbucks gift cards. The charming European decor is exceptionally comfortable. Check out the Something to Bark About package, which includes a welcome bag equipped with toys, treats, food, spring water, food bowls, and of course, baggies. No fee. 25-pound weight limit.

Harbor Court Hotel
(866) 792-6283
165 Steuart St
(between Howard & Mission sts)
San Francisco, California 94105
www.harborcourthotel.com
Price Range: $$$

Located in the YMCA in a space that formerly held dorm-style rooms featuring bunk beds and one bath per floor, the Harbor Court Hotel's funky Roman-gone-Eastern decor offers all the warmth and comfort Kimpton hotels are known for. The cozy rooms come standard with high-speed Internet access and amazing views of the bay. Hotel perks include complimentary evening wine hour and in-room 24-hour televised yoga instruction as well as use of the YMCA's Olympic-size pool and rooftop jogging track. Legendary Ozumo sushi, Ponzu, Café Pescatore and Postrio are all in the neighborhood. Dog amenities include a bed, water bowl, toys and a list of dog-friendly restaurants and parks. 50-pound weight limit.

Hotel Monaco: San Francisco
(866) 622-5284
501 Geary St
(@ Taylor St)
San Francisco, California 94102
www.monaco-sf.com
Price Range: $$$$
The French-inspired Hotel Monaco is dazzling. The plush guestrooms—with stripes, patterns and twirls going every which way—are divine. Guest perks include complimentary morning town car service within the financial district, on-site Spa Equilibrium, a fitness center and complimentary evening wine hour, complete with tarot card readings and chair massage. If you'd like some quiet company, the hotel will provide you with a goldfish during your stay. Dog offerings include the Bone-A-Petite package, with chew toys, dog cookies, a mat and towel, plus a bowl filled with mountain spring water. The concierge can arrange pet-sitting or dog walking. No fee. No size limit.

Hotel Palomar
(866) 373-4941
12 4th St
(between Market & Mission sts)
San Francisco, California 94103
www.hotelpalomar.com
Price Range: $$$$
This boutique Kimpton hotel barely opened before landing on

Condé Nast Traveler's Gold List and *Travel & Leisure's* Top 500 Hotels in the World list. Offering a quiet sanctuary five floors above the commotion at Union Square, the Palomar—with its '40s French, almost-electric decor—is as inviting as it is unique. The Rene Magritte suite offers the bluest, cloud-filled ceiling you can imagine. Other perks include designated rooms for taller guests as well as a bath menu for guests staying in suites. The hotel's award-winning French restaurant, 5th Floor, forgoes the signature leopard-print carpeting in favor of a zebra print. Dog services available upon request. The 25-pound weight limit is somewhat flexible. No fee.

Hotel Triton
(800) 800-1299
342 Grant Ave
(@ Harlan St)
San Francisco, California 94108
www.hoteltriton.com
Price Range: $$$
Welcome to Atlantis, Kimpton style! Celebrity suites include the Jerry Garcia suite, designed by the man himself, and the Black Magic Bedroom by Carlos Santana. Other offerings include the Zen Den and Eco Rooms. Perks include a 24-hour yoga channel in guestrooms, freshly baked cookies and a nightly wine and beer party, with tarot card readings and chair massage, plus a DJ on Friday nights. Dog amenities include personalized dog bowls, as well as beds. Pups can also receive grooming or a pet manicure coordinated through the hotel. The only real rule is that your dog must be crated if you leave her alone in the room. No fees. No weight limit.

Mandarin Oriental: San Francisco
(800) 622-0404
222 Sansome St
(between Pine & California sts)
San Francisco, California 94104

www.mandarinoriental.com/hotel/519000001.asp
Price Range: $$$$$
Always on all of the *Travel & Leisure* and *Condé Nast* best-
hotel lists, the Mandarin Oriental offers superb panoramic
views as well as a level of tranquility that can only be found in
the finest Eastern hotels. Pet amenities include food and water
bowls and gourmet treats. The Mandarin's location, in the
heart of the financial district, does not make it particularly
conducive to leisurely walks. However, the off-leash Alamo
Square is a short cab ride away. And for your sans-dog outings,
the hotel's exceptionally accommodating staff will coordinate
pet care for you. There is a $25 per-day charge. 20-pound
weight limit. One pet per room.

Monticello Inn
(866) 778-6169
127 Ellis St
(between Powell & Cyril Magnum sts)
San Francisco, California 94102
www.monticelloinn.com
Price Range: $$$
Bringing Colonial Virginia to San Francisco, the Monticello Inn
is situated in a landmark building that dates back to 1906. Its
Union Square address means you will have plenty of shops
and restaurants within walking distance. In honor of Thomas
Jefferson, and his love for books, the hotel has teamed up with
Border Books to offer bestselling books in the honor bar of
their suites. Other perks include weekly book readings by
local authors as well as an evening wine hour. For your pup,
the hotel provides welcome treats, bowls, a placemat and a
list of nearby dog-friendly spots—including several restaurants.
Just ask for the Pet's Getaway package. 50-pound weight limit.
No fees.

Palace Hotel
(415) 512-1111
2 New Montgomery St
(between Annie & 2nd sts)
San Francisco, California 94105
www.sfpalace.com
Price Range: $$$$

The luxuriant 19th-century Palace Hotel may have catered to presidents and royalty in the past, but this is a new millennium and it's definitely become a place for the whole family, dogs included. The hotel boasts Maxfields restaurant and the famous Pied Piper Bar, which offers the best-ranked martini in the city. Other hotel amenities include a sky-lit swimming pool, a sauna, fitness center and full-service business center. The staff will supply you with a list of pet-friendly stores and services in the neighborhood. The hotel offers food and water bowls. However, other amenities are up to you. There is an 80-pound weight limit. A $100 deposit, as well as advance notice, is required.

The Prescott Hotel
(866) 271-3632
545 Post St
(between Mason & Taylor sts)
San Francisco, California 94102
www.prescotthotel.com
Price Range: $$$

Recently named one of the Best Value Hotels by *Travel & Leisure*, the Prescott goes above and beyond to accommodate guests and their pets in any way possible. This hotel offers all of the usual standout Kimpton amenities. However, the decor is more understated-regal than Kimpton's signature collision of Renaissance colors and patterns. Standard amenities include morning town car service within the financial district, wireless Internet throughout the hotel and preferential treatment at Wolfgang Puck's adjacent restaurant, Postrio. Club level guests also have a separate concierge and lounge, as well as complimentary continental breakfast and evening cocktail hour. No Fee. No weight limit.

The Ritz-Carlton: San Francisco
(415) 296-7465
600 Stockton St
(between California & Stockton sts)
San Francisco, California 94108
www.ritzcarlton.com/hotels/san_francisco
Price Range: $$$$$
A Nob Hill landmark within walking distance of Fisherman's Wharf, the San Francisco Ritz is the only hotel in North America to receive Mobil's five-star and AAA's five-diamond honors for both their hotel and dining room. With their VIP (Very Important Pooch) program, it's clear the Ritz aims to surpass all expectations in the pet category as well. Among the amenities are in-room dining (fat-free, raw chopped-beef tenderloin with sliced baby carrots), Fido's cookies, a Windsor dog bed, a bowl and a placemat. There's even a Pooch Pack with information about nearby dog offerings, including parks and stores, plus a bedtime story for your dog. $125 fee. 10-pound weight limit.

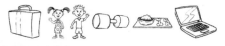

Serrano Hotel
(866) 289-6561
405 Taylor St
(@ O' Farrell St)
San Francisco, California 94102
www.serranohotel.com
Price Range: $$$
Check in is a bit of a gamble at the luxe, Spanish-style Serrano. Play a hand of blackjack at the reception desk and win a free upgrade. If you lose, the hotel will ask for a $5 donation for the San Francisco SPCA. With stakes like that, you really can't lose. Though this Kimpton hotel supplies a dog bowl for water, doggie biscuits and cleanup bags, you'll be charged for extra dog

food, a pet bed or leash. The hotel can arrange dog walking and pet-sitting. No fee. Small dogs only.

The Sir Francis Drake
(800) 795-7129
450 Powell St
(@ Sutter St)
San Francisco, California 94102
www.sirfrancisdrake.com
Price Range: $$$
Near MOMA and the Moscone center, this 1930s boutique hotel overlooks Union Square. The ornate chandeliers, crown molding and striped wallpaper add to the big band-era ambience. But the real time warp is on the 21st floor at the flapper-glam nightclub, Harry Denton's Starlight Room, where the live orchestra plays a mix of swing and Motown. Scala's Bistro, their award-winning restaurant offers Italian and French cuisine, but if all you want is a quick bite, Caffe Espresso is a good bet. The hotel also has a gym and business center. The Bowzer Buddy package includes a bowl, chew toy and a guide to dog-friendly walks in San Francisco. No fee. No weight limit.

Tuscan Inn at Fisherman's Wharf
(800) 648-4626
425 N Point St
(between Mason & Taylor sts)
San Francisco, California 94133
www.tuscaninn.com
Price Range: $$$
This quaint hotel is close to many San Francisco attractions, including Pier 39, Ghiradelli Square and Fort Mason. The ambiance is more floral Victorian wallpaper than the stated Italian boutique, but you'll find the pleasing Café Pescatore downstairs along with afternoon coffee and biscotti in the lobby. If you're in town for business, the hotel offers limousine

service three times daily to the financial district. Your pup is allowed at Pier 39, and at several nearby dog parks, but not alone in your room. Your options are to get a pet-sitter or crate him while you are out. $25 fee. No weight limit.

Villa Florence
(800) 553-4411
225 Powell St
(between Geary & O' Farrell sts)
San Francisco, California 94102
www.villaflorence.com
Price Range: $$$
It's near impossible not to feel at home in this luxury Kimpton boutique hotel, which offers family-style Italian hospitality along with Italian Renaissance decor. Perks include the Kimpton's standard complimentary evening wine reception, wireless Internet access, 24/7 laundry access, as well as Aveda bath products. Villa Florence does not have a restaurant. However, numerous pet-friendly cafes are within walking distance of the hotel's Union Square address. The Villa's restaurant of choice is the adjacent Kuletos, which serves Italian cuisine. The concierge will arrange for pet-sitting. No fee. Small dogs only.

W: San Francisco
(415) 777-5300
181 3rd St
(@ Howard St)
San Francisco, California 94103
www.starwood.com/whotels/sanfrancisco
Price Range: $$$$
Modern and a bit cheeky, this W could easily pass for the Pottery Barn's naughty little sister. Plush beds, sexy music throughout the hotel and the hot XYZ bar draw quite a crowd. The three-story lobby has couches for sprawling on, built-in board games, and a heated patio that gets a little rowdy after

hours. The signature Whatever/Whenever button on all the hotel phones allows for fulfillment of any request you can think of. Other perks include a fitness center, pool and massage services. Your pup receives a welcome pack, a bed, tag and baggies, and any referrals you might need. $25 fee per night, $100 cleaning fee. 50-pound weight limit.

The Westin: St. Francis
(415) 397-7000
335 Powell St
(between Post & Geary sts)
San Francisco, California 94102
www.starwood.com/westin/stfrancis
Price Range: $$$
With cable cars coming as close as the hotel's front door, the St. Francis and its distinct red awnings have been a city staple for a century. You're right by the park at dog-friendly Union Square—which features street entertainers, art exhibitions and the occasional free concert. If you make arrangements before arriving, the hotel will have its signature Heavenly Dog Bed ready for your pup. Meals and treats as well as dog-walking and pet-sitting services are also available. Your amenities include high-speed Internet access, a hotel coffee bar and two on-site restaurants—one casual, one elegant. No fee, 40-pound weight limit.

(707) – Calistoga, Healdsburg & Yountville

Calistoga Ranch
(800) 942-4220
580 Lommel Rd
(off Silverado Trl)
Calistoga, California 94515
www.calistogaranch.com
Price Range: $$$$$

The tree house reaches a whole new level with the indoor/out-door accommodations at this elegant resort in northern Napa. The 47 individual guest lodges come complete with an out-door living room, situated on a large private deck. Calistoga promises world-class dining, wine tasting, a five-star spa and stunning vistas. The bathhouse offers hot mineral water pools, yoga classes on the deck and heavenly spa treatments. Other amazing offerings include a heated pool, where you can take in the lovely outdoor fireplace or the unbelievable view; a wine cave; and hiking trails. Dog perks include three sizes of dog beds, bowls, biscuits and toys. No fees. No weight limit.

Hotel Healdsburg
(707) 431-2800
25 Matheson St
(@ Healdsburg Ave)
Healdsburg, California 95448
www.slh.com/healdsburg
Price Range: $$$$
This minimalist-chic hotel has everything you need, including a gourmet restaurant, a noteworthy wine cellar and spa servic-es for those not content to soak in the six-foot tubs. The pictur-esque town of Healdsburg is perfect for afternoon and evening walks around the plaza with your dog. And some of the near-by wineries—after all, you are in Sonoma—allow dogs to tag along, but be sure to call first. The Healdsburg welcomes dogs 15 pounds or less. $150 flat fee.

Vintage Inn
(800) 351-1133
6541 Washington St
(between Washington & Humboldt sts)
Yountville, California 94559
www.vintageinn.com
Price Range: $$$$$

If you love Provence but can't venture to France, check into the Vintage Inn, a *Travel & Leisure* Best 500 Hotels in the World pick for 2004. This romantic chateau in Napa offers champagne breakfasts and afternoon tea. The guestrooms, which offer fireplaces and sunken tubs, are perfectly romantic without being ornate. For a $30 fee, your pup can come along, and the staff will supply him with a bag of treats. Leashed dogs are welcome to wander the property and nearby parks. The local pet shop, Best Friends, offers walking and pet-sitting services. Several wineries and restaurants with patios allow small dogs, but call ahead before bringing your dog.

(510) – Newark

W: Silicon Valley – Newark
(510) 494-8800
8200 Gateway Blvd
(@ Thornton Ave)
Newark, California 94560
www.starwood.com/whotels.siliconvalley
Price Range: $$$$
In the heart of Silicon Valley, the W hotel brings city chic to the suburbs. Stones abound in the swank decor, with Zen-inducing candles and wood, juxtaposed to rich, plush fabrics. Catering to business travelers, the hotel also offers plenty of amenities for Bay Area adventurers, including a pool, complete with a small strip of sand and a fire pit. Shopping is nearby, and there are plenty of dog-friendly outdoor offerings, including beaches, hiking, dog parks, trails and marshlands. Dog amenities include a welcome package (toy, gourmet treat, W Hotel pet tag and cleanup bags), in-room dog necessities and essential service referrals. Pet rates are $25 a night, with a nonrefundable $100 cleaning fee.

(650) - Half Moon Bay, Palo Alto & Redwood City

The Ritz-Carlton: Half Moon Bay
(650) 712-7000
1 Miramontes Point Rd
(@ Pacific Coast Hwy)
Half Moon Bay, California 94019
www.ritz-carlton.com/resorts/half_moon_bay
Price Range: $$$$$

Your dog can run along the Pacific shores just outside this picturesque seaside hotel situated 45 minutes from the Golden
Gate Bridge. The architecture and decor is reminiscent of the
northeast, but the yoga studio and coed candlelit Roman bath
are all Californian. The Ritz will set you up with its favorite
dog walking service, Yuppy Puppy, while you enjoy the hotels
activities, including whale watching, on the beach horseback
riding or a pumpkin body peel at the 16,000-square-foot spa.
Your pup is welcome at the boutique-antique town of Half
Moon Bay, but not in the hotel lobby or guest areas. $125 fee.
30-pound weight limit.

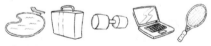

Sofitel: San Francisco Bay
(650) 598-9000
223 Twin Dolphin Dr
(@ Shoreline Dr)
Redwood City, California 94065
www.sofitel.com
Price Range: $$$

The staff of this Silicon Valley hotel goes out of their way to
make you and your pet comfortable, doling out treats to all
well-behaved pups that come through the door. Your dog is
free to roam the lush grounds, and join you for a walk around
the blue lagoon or on the hotel's jogging track. Dog walking is
also available upon request. But your pup must stay on dry
land if you take a dip in the heated pool. The hotel also offers

a fitness center and conference facilities. A golf course and tennis courts are within walking distance.

The Westin: Palo Alto
(650) 321-4422
675 El Camino Real
(between Embarcadero & University sts)
Palo Alto, California 94301
www.starwood.com/westin/paloalto
Price Range: $$$
The Westin Palo Alto sits across the street from the Stanford University campus, offering ample space for dog-walking. The Westin's signature Heavenly Dog Bed will be ready for your pup if you give the hotel advance notice. Shopping, restaurants and Palo Alto nightlife are within walking distance. The hotel offers deep-tissue massage and aromatherapy; courtyard views from every room; in addition to the upscale Restaurant Soleil, which serves up Mediterranean cuisine. No fee. 80-pound weight limit.

The Westin: San Francisco Airport
(650) 692-3500
1 Old Bayshore Hwy
(@ E Millbrae Ave)
Millbrae, California 94030
www.starwood.com/westin/sanfrancisco
Price Range: $$$
The rooms at this Westin are soundproof, a nice touch near an airport. Other creature comforts include an indoor pool, on-site fitness center, high-speed Internet and Alfiere's serving Mediterranean fare. Traffic permitting, downtown San Francisco and Silicon Valley are a half-hour drive away. A three-mile trail starts outside the lobby, providing a perfect spot for an evening walk with your dog. If you give the hotel staff advance notice, a dog bed will be awaiting your pup. No fee. 50-pound weight limit.

(408) - Cupertino

Cypress Hotel
(800) 499-1408
10050 S De Anza Blvd
(between Cali Ave & Stevens Creek Blvd)
Cupertino, California 95014
www.thecypresshotel.com
Price Range: $$$$

Mediterranean style and modern technology merge in this luxe Silicon Valley hotel that offers amenities for both business and leisure travelers. From the divine outdoor colonnade and the plush living room—complete with fireplace—to the polka dot wallpaper and plush animal-print fabrics, this Kimpton hotel does not disappoint. Pay a little extra for the See Spot Run package and the hotel will stock your room with dog bowls, treats, toys and souvenir dog tags. The concierge has a list of dog-friendly restaurants, as well as referrals for local dog walkers and pet-sitters. The Cypress asks that you crate your dog when he is alone in the room. No fee. No weight limit.

Maple Tree Inn
(408) 720-9700
711 E El Camino Real
(@ S Fair Oaks Ave)
Sunnyvale, California 94087
www.mapletreeinn.com
Price Range: $$$$

Value-savvy business travelers will love the modern conveniences of this relaxing retreat in the heart of Silicon Valley. The Maple Tree Inn is exactly what you would expect of a hotel with this name: Harvest-themed accents add to an exceedingly comfortable setting. Pet amenities include pet treats and a cozy blanket. Your dog is welcome to roam on leash around the beautiful outdoor landscape, which offers plenty of green space. For trails and hiking, visit Stevens Creek in the foothills of the Santa Cruz Mountains. A nearby dog park in Palo Alto offers space for off-leash play. No fee. No weight limit.

The Westin: Santa Clara
(408) 986-0700
5101 Great American Pkwy
(@ Tasman Dr)
Santa Clara, California 95054
www.starwood.com/westin/santaclara
Price Range: $$$
This Silicon Valley Westin is made for the business traveler. The Santa Clara Convention Center is next door, and the hotel provides high-speed Internet access and translation services within the business center. Also nearby is Paramount's Great American Theme Park, as is the Municipal Golf and Tennis club and a dog-friendly walking trail. Other perks include an outdoor heated pool, a fitness center and a whirlpool. The Tresca restaurant offers California cuisine, or you can get a quick bite at the Lobby Lounge. The hotel provides your pup a dog version of their signature Heavenly bed. $50 fee, 40-pound weight limit.

Southern California

(310) - Los Angeles

Beverly Hills
Avalon Beverly Hills
Beverly Hills Hotel & Bungalows
Beverly Hills Hotels & Bungalows
Beverly Hilton
L'Ermitage Beverly Hills
The Peninsula: Beverly Hills
The Regent: Beverly Wilshire

Los Angeles
Four Seasons Hotel: Los Angeles - Beverly Hills
Hotel Bel Air
Le Meridien: Beverly Hills
Sofitel: Los Angeles
St. Regis: Los Angeles
W: Los Angeles
The Westin: Century Plaza Hotel & Spa
The Westin: Los Angeles Airport

Marina del Rey
The Ritz-Carlton: Marina del Rey

Santa Monica
Le Merigot Marriott
Viceroy Santa Monica

(323) - West Hollywood
Chateau Marmont

(213) - Los Angeles
The Westin: Bonaventure Hotel & Suites

(626) - Pasadena

The Ritz-Carlton: Huntington Hotel & Spa
The Westin: Pasadena

(562) - Long Beach

The Westin: Long Beach

(949) - Orange County

St. Regis: Monarch Beach
Four Seasons Hotel: Newport Beach

(714) - Costa Mesa

The Westin: South Coast Plaza

(760) - Palm Springs & Carlsbad

La Quinta Resort & Club
The Westin: Mission Hills Resort
Four Seasons Hotel: Aviara, North San Diego

(858) - La Jolla & Rancho Santa Fe

La Valencia
The Inn at Rancho Santa Fe

(619) - San Diego

W: San Diego
The Westin: Horton Plaza

(805) - Santa Barbara

Four Seasons Resort: Santa Barbara
San Ysidro Ranch

(310) - Beverly Hills

Avalon Beverly Hills

(800) 670-6183
9400 West Olympic Blvd
(between Olympic Blvd & Beverly Dr)
Beverly Hills, California 90212
www.avalonbeverlyhills.com
Price Range: $$$$$

Retro minimalism meets Eastern serene at this south-of-Wilshire Beverly Hills hotel that was once home to Marilyn Monroe. The Avalon doesn't go overboard on amenities but they do supply water and dog biscuits. The concierge is happy to connect you with local dog-sitting services and groomers, and to point you in the direction of nearby parks. In this area, it's not unusual to see pets on the patios of many restaurants, or taking a ride in the sling-bag of a local fashionista. Even in stores that don't officially welcome pets, most salespeople will look the other way. The Viceroy in Santa Monica is the Avalon's sister hotel. $150 deposit. 20-pound weight limit.

Beverly Hills Hotel & Bungalows

(800) 283-8885
9641 Sunset Blvd
(@ N Beverly Dr)
Beverly Hills, California 90210
www.beverlyhillshotel.com
Price Range: $$$$$

There's no better place for your pup to rub shoulders with the dogs of the rich and famous than the Beverly Hills Hotel. A longtime celebrity magnet, the pink palace really rolls out the red carpet for canines. Dog perks include a dog bed, water bowls, tennis balls and biscuits with your pup's name spelled out in signature pink icing. Just like other guests, dogs are greeted by name during their stay. Guests with dogs are restricted to the bungalows with private patios. However, these are among the hotel's most luxurious accommodations, so it shouldn't cramp your style. 30-pound weight limit. $200 fee.

Beverly Hilton
(310) 274-7777
9876 Wilshire Blvd
(between Santa Monica & Wilshire blvds)
Beverly Hills, California 90210
www.hilton.com/hotels/LAXBHHH
Price Range: $$$$
The Beverly Hills outpost of the Hilton—home of the Golden Globe awards ceremony—far exceeds this chain's reputation for superior, if corporate, amenities and service. With an airline desk, salon, barber shop, florist, clothing and gift shops, plus a business center and full administrative support, this Hilton could be an island unto itself. However, it would be silly to stay in all the time when the hotel is within walking distance of the glitz and glamour of Rodeo Drive. There are no specific dog amenities, but the staff can direct you to one of the many nearby groomers, sitters, pet spas and boutiques. 25-pound weight limit. $25 a day with a maximum of $100 per stay.

Four Seasons Hotel: Los Angeles - Beverly Hills
(310) 273-2222
300 S Doheny Dr (@ W 3rd St)
Los Angeles, California 90048
www.fourseasons.com/losangeles
Price Range: $$$$$
The Four Seasons Los Angeles is everything you might expect a luxury hotel in Beverly Hills to be: glamorous, accommodating and not without the requisite only-in-LA spa treatments. The ambiance is part tropical island, part executive boardroom, with elegant rooms and beautiful views. There's a heated pool, a fitness center with trainers and a private cabana for spa services. You can try the California Sunset or Body Bronzing Massage, or the Oxyliance Cellular Facial. The hotel

restaurant, Gardens, offers Asian-inspired cuisine, and the Café serves Mediterranean fare. Rodeo is close by, as are tennis facilities and golf courses.

Hotel Bel Air
(800) 648-4097
701 Stone Canyon Rd
(between Chalon Rd & Tortuoso Way)
Los Angeles, California 90077
www.hotelbelair.com
Price Range: $$$$$
It does not get much better than this five-star, five-diamond Bel Air Hotel. Once a favorite of Grace Kelly and Cary Grant, this posh hideaway with private guestroom entrances has become a sanctuary for privacy-starved celebrities. The expansive grounds include lush gardens and a swan pond. Renovated in 2000, the exquisite decor has a residential feel. The bathrooms, guestrooms and pool have also been taken to the next level. A dog goodie bag with a toy, rawhide bones, food, biscuits and bowl are available at check-in. The concierge can arrange pet-sitting and dog walking if you'd like to try the hotel's famous Sunday brunch. $300 fee. 30-pound limit.

L'Ermitage Beverly Hills
(800) 800-2113
9291 Burton Way (@ Foothill Rd)
Beverly Hills, California 91210
www.lermitagehotel.com
Price Range: $$$$$
A five-star, five-diamond hotel, L'Ermitage is a constant at, or very near, the top of every best-hotel list there is. Exquisitely understated, this French-gone-Eastern hotel combines high-tech amenities with a sublime minimalist decor. Rooms come standard with private balconies, sliding wood screens, plus high-speed Internet and "smart" lighting and climate control. The resident restaurant JAAN and the Writer's Bar are destinations in their own right. Your dog can dine on the Pet

Companion Menu, which includes tuna tartar with anchovy, foie gras with micro-farmed chicken eggs and beluga caviar. Other offerings include the Raffles' spa, the fitness center, the rooftop pool and the steam room. $150 fee. 40-pound weight limit.

Le Meridien: Beverly Hills
(310) 247-0400
465 S La Cienega Blvd
(@ N San Vicente Blvd)
Los Angeles, California 90048
www.beverlyhills.lemeridien.com
Price Range: $$$$
If you love shopping, this elegant, European-style hotel is the place to stay. The hotel sits on La Cienega's Eastern-bent restaurant row and is just a short drive from Rodeo Drive, the Beverly Center, the Grove and the Farmers' Market, where your pup can sample treats at the Three Dog Bakery. If you feel like venturing out solo, the hotel staff will coordinate dog-walking and pet-sitting services. While the hotel doesn't offer dog-specific amenities, the nearby Chateau Marmutt pampers dogs with aromatherapy grooming. People perks include the hotel's health club and outdoor pool. No fee for the first three days, then $25 per day. 50-pound weight limit.

Le Merigot Marriott
(310) 395-9700
1740 Ocean Ave
(between Pico & Colorado blvds)
Santa Monica, California 90401
www.lemerigothotel.com
Price Range: $$$$$
With an award-winning spa and restaurant, Le Merigot is a haven of French tranquility, complete with ocean views—steps away from the world-famous Santa Monica Pier. The pier is dog paradise, and the Third Street Promenade—where you'll

find an earthy mix of fine dining, eclectic shops and bizarre street entertainment—is right across Ocean Avenue. The hotel's Club Meg pet-friendly program provides plenty of dog amenities as well as gourmet in-room dining services. Their only requirement: Dogs must be people-friendly and leashed when in public. There is a $150 deposit, a $35 cleaning fee. No weight limit.

The Peninsula: Beverly Hills
(800) 462-7899
9882 S Santa Monica Blvd
(southwest of Wilshire Blvd)
Beverly Hills, California 90210
www.beverlyhills.peninsula.com
Price Range: $$$$$
This five-star, five-diamond suite and villa hotel has received countless honors, including the number-one spot on *Andrew Harper's Hideaway Report* of the Top 20 City Hotels. Offerings include chauffeured Rolls Royce service, perfect for a trip to the Getty or nearby Rodeo Drive; and their renowned five-star rooftop spa, complete with a lap pool, anti-aging treatments and massage services. Foodies will appreciate the award-winning Belvedere restaurant. If you're in a hurry, try Pen Air Meals, the Peninsula's gourmet to go. With advance notice, the hotel will greet your pup by name and provide her with a deluxe dog bed and biscuits. Pet sitters are also available. $35 per night fee. No weight limit.

The Regent: Beverly Wilshire
(310) 275-5200
9500 Wilshire Blvd
(between Carmelita Ave & N Santa Monica Blvd)
Beverly Hills, California 90212
www.regenthotels.com/beverlywilshire
Price Range: $$$$$

This romantic Rodeo Drive hotel lets you choose your own decor—the classic Wilshire wing or the contemporary Beverly Wing, but either way you'll find yourself wondering if you're on a movie set. The ambiance is old-Hollywood, more cigars and mahogany than yoga and wheat grass. The Dining Room has California cuisine, and The Bar is a celeb hot spot. Other perks include a steam room, massage services and a pass to Sports Club/LA. For your dog, the Regent provides bones, personalized bowls as well as dog walking: $25 for 30 minutes or $75 for a canyon hike. No fee. 15-pound weight limit.

The Ritz-Carlton: Marina del Rey
(310) 823-1700
4375 Admiralty Way
(@ Bali Way)
Marina del Rey, California 90292
www.ritzcarlton.com/hotels/marina_del_rey
Price Range: $$$$$
This AAA Five Diamond waterfront hotel features elegant European decor and magnificent views of the marina. Walk a mile to watch the pageant of non-conformity at the Venice Beach boardwalk, awash in street entertainment, cheesy souvenir shops, pumped-up bodybuilders and political activists. For a more sedate adventure, try Fisherman's Village, about a mile in the other direction, or just wander around one of the world's largest marinas, only steps away. The concierge can arrange for dog-walking services. There is $125 fee that's good for seven days; after which, an additional $125 charge applies. 30-pound weight limit.

St. Regis: Los Angeles
(310) 277-6111
2055 Avenue of the Stars
(@ W Olympic Blvd)
Los Angeles, California 90067
www.starwood.com/stregis/losangeles
Price Range: $$$$$

This towering Century City hotel offers guests balcony views that for the most part do not exist in Los Angeles. The atmosphere is old-school elegant, with all the proper services and amenities never more than a phone call away. A doggie welcome pack is presented at check-in and includes a silver dog dish, gourmet dog food, bottled water and a large, plush dog bed. The dog room-service menu offers everything from filet mignon to fish. The concierge will coordinate pet care. The St. Regis allows dogs anywhere on the premises except in the restaurant. The dog-friendly, open-air Century City Mall is only short walk from the hotel. There is a $25 flat fee per dog.

Sofitel: Los Angeles
(310) 278-5444
8555 Beverly Blvd
(@ La Cienega Blvd)
Los Angeles, California 90048
www.sofitel.com
Price Range: $$$
The staff here is attentive and eager to please, and the country-style rooms are big enough for you and your pet. Whether you're here for business or pleasure, you'll find everything you need in close proximity. The hotel offers a fitness center with trainers, an outdoor pool and a business center. The Getty Center, LACMA and downtown Los Angeles are under 30 minutes away, and Rodeo Drive and the Sunset strip are even closer. If you're feeling energetic you can hike your pup at nearby Runyon Canyon, or you can always take advantage of the scores of dog day-care facilities in the neighborhood. No fees. No weight limit.

Viceroy Santa Monica
(800) 670-6185
819 Ocean Ave (@ Pico Blvd)
Santa Monica, California 90401

www.viceroysantamonica.com
Price Range: $$$$

The exquisitely minimalist Viceroy, sister hotel of the uber-hip Avalon in Beverly Hills, offers you Pacific ocean views, two pools, a bustling night scene in the lobby bar and spa services (in-room or poolside) courtesy of Fred Segal. They don't offer much in the way of dog amenities, but the close proximity to Santa Monica's best dog park means plenty of play for your dog. (Beware of the rangers: They are quick to ticket you if your dog doesn't have a Santa Monica license.) If you're game for a drive up the PCH, there are a couple of unofficial dog-friendly beaches. The Viceroy accepts small dogs only with a $100 fee.

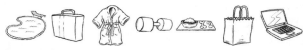

W: Los Angeles
(310) 208-8765
930 Hilgard Ave
(@ Le Conte Ave)
Los Angeles, California 90024
www.starwood.com/whotels/losangeles
Price Range: $$$$

Part librarian and part rock star, this W knows how to cater to every guest. From the waterfall-inspired front stairs to the high-tech meeting rooms, you'll find W quirks all around—like white pencils and black paper in the meeting rooms, or best-selling novels shelved in the lobby, ready for perusal. The 24-hour gym has in-house trainers at your service, and you can get a peel, facial, massage or mani-pedi any time of day. Mojo, featuring Latin-American cuisine, serves poolside, or you can grab a quick bite at the W: Café. Pet amenities include toys, treats, tags, baggies, beds, bowls and a Pet in Room sign. $25 per night, $100 fee. No weight limit.

The Westin: Century Plaza Hotel & Spa

(310) 277-2000
2025 Avenue of the Stars
(@ Constellation & Pico blvds)
Los Angeles, California 90067
www.starwood.com/westin/centuryplaza

Price Range: $$$$

This Beverly Hills-adjacent, Century City hotel, known for its series of shimmering pools, is a longtime dining and recreational haven for both presidents and Hollywood celebrities. It's a haven for your dog too, with grassy areas set aside for lounging and walking. As long as your pet's leashed, he's welcome in the lobby. One place the dog can't go, but you'll want to check out: the 35,000-square-foot spa with saunas, eucalyptus steam and massage. 50-pound weight limit, $30 per night fee.

The Westin: Los Angeles Airport

(310) 216-5858
5400 W Century Blvd
(@ Airport & Century aves)
Los Angeles, California 90045
www.starwood.com/westin/losangeles

Price Range: $$$

Dog pampering begins upon arrival at the Westin LAX. A Doggie Welcome Kit, which includes meals, treats, bowls and a Westin Heavenly Dog Bed—awaits your pet. As for you, the hotel restaurant, Charisma, serves continental cuisine, and the Lobby Court offers a pool table and local jazz bands on Wednesday nights. If you want to give your pet her own getaway while you're enjoying all that jazz, the nearby Kennel Club has boarding. Tell them you're staying at the Westin, and you'll get a discount. No fee. 40-pound weight limit.

(323) – West Hollywood

Chateau Marmont

(323) 656-1010
8221 Sunset Blvd (@ Crescent Heights Blvd)
West Hollywood, California 90046
www.chateaumarmont.com
Price Range: $$$$$
Gazing down on L.A.'s famed Sunset Strip, the Chateau
Marmot has been a celebrity retreat since the 1920s. You can
walk the same halls as Greta Garbo, Humphrey Bogart,
Marilyn Monroe, John Belushi, James Dean and Robert
DeNiro. Architecturally, the hotel is a replica of the 18th century Loire Chateau Amboise, down to the ivy-covered pillars,
gothic vaulted ceilings in the lobby and lush swimming pool.
Each of the ten deluxe rooms is styled differently, adding to the
boutique feel. Other perks include a fitness and business center. Adjacent to the hotel is the Bar Marmont, a hot spot for
celebrity sightings. $100 fee. 60-pound weight limit.

(213) – Los Angeles

The Westin: Bonaventure Hotel & Suites

(213) 624-1000
404 S Figueroa St (@ Flower St)
Los Angeles, California 90071
www.starwood.com/westin/bonaventure
Price Range: $$$
The largest convention hotel in Los Angeles, this Westin
boasts 35 floors and a six-story shopping atrium that features
more than 40 shops and restaurants. Its rooftop steakhouse,
L.A. Prime, offers city views, as well as the popular revolving
cocktail lounge, BonaVista. Your dog's welcome to walk
throughout the hotel and shopping areas, as long as she's
leashed. For outside activity, there's a small park across the
street. However, a leash is required there too. If you need

dog-walking or pet-sitting services, the concierge will set you up. No fee. 40-pound weight limit.

(626) - Pasadena

The Ritz-Carlton: Huntington Hotel & Spa

(626) 568-3900
1401 S Oak Knoll Ave (@ Hillcrest Ave)
Pasadena, California 91106
www.ritzcarlton.com/hotels/huntington
Price Range: $$$$$

A Pasadena landmark since 1907, the Ritz-Carlton Huntington is a relaxation sanctuary. With over two-dozen treatment rooms, the full-service spa offers massages, facials and body exfoliation services. Foodies take note: *Gourmet* magazine recently honored the hotel's dining rooms as one of the world's best. You can take your dog on a leashed walk through the hotel's 23-acre property that includes a Pasadena must-see: the famed Picture Bridge, overlooking the hotel's Japanese gardens, replete with paintings of California landmarks. You are within walking distance of dog-friendly Old Town Pasadena, which offers 130 shops in revamped century-old buildings. $125 fee. 30-pound weight limit.

The Westin: Pasadena

(626) 792-2727
191 N Los Robles Ave (@ E Walnut St)
Pasadena, California 91101
www.starwood.com/westin/pasadena
Price Range: $$$

This Westin mixes traditional elegance with a splash of color, featuring mosaic-tiled fountains, hot tubs, a heated outdoor pool and a state-of-the-art fitness center. The Westin's restaurant, Oaks, serves California cuisine. The hotel is ideally located near shopping in historic Old Town Pasadena—where you can pick up some treats at Three Dog Bakery—and dog-friendly Memorial Park. Visit on the right summer night, and you and your pup can enjoy a free concert at one of the most beautiful band shells on the West Coast. Your pup is provided with Westin's Heavenly Dog Bed, the miniature version of their signature Heavenly Bed. No fee. 30-pound weight limit.

(562) - Long Beach

The Westin: Long Beach

(562) 436-3000
333 E Ocean Blvd (between Elm Ave & Long Beach Blvd)
Long Beach, California 90802
www.starwood.com/westin/longbeach
Price Range: $$$
As far as dog-friendly towns go, Long Beach is the ultimate. And this convention center-adjacent Westin welcomes pups. Leashed dogs are allowed in the lobby and on hotel grounds but not in the hotel's Centennial Ballroom: The city's largest, accommodates up to 1,500 people. The dog beach is nearby, and a public walking trail frequented by joggers and bikers starts two blocks away. Catalina's a one-hour ferry ride away, and as long as she's crated, your dog can tag along free of charge. For local dog news and events, check out hautedogs.org, run by local dog activist Justin Rudd. No fee. 50-pound weight limit.

(949) - Orange County

Four Seasons Hotel: Newport Beach

(949) 759-0808
690 Newport Center Dr (@ Santa Cruz Dr)
Newport Beach, California 92660

www.fourseasons.com/newportbeach
Price Range: $$$$$

The requisite Four Seasons elegance notwithstanding, this breezy beach-style hotel is laid back enough for a bathing suit and flip flops, high-tech enough to furnish every set of lounge chairs with data ports and phones, and yet romantic enough to have an outdoor poolside fireplace. You can play golf overlooking the Pacific on the Tom Fazio-designed championship course. The hotel also boasts an outdoor fitness center with trainers, a pool bar, lighted tennis courts, and a spa featuring massages and facials. Your pup gets treats, bones, bowls and a sleeping pad upon arrival. And Fashion Island, the open-air mall adjacent to the hotel, is dog friendly. No fee. 25-pound weight limit.

St. Regis: Monarch Beach

(800) 722-1543
1 Monarch Beach Resort
(off Niguel Rd)
Dana Point, California 92629
www.stregismb.com
Price Range: $$$$$

Elegant and genteel, the suites in the St. Regis could have been lifted right out of *Town & Country*. You can sun at the beach or pool, both are right outside your door. There's plenty for everyone: the Sandcastle Kids Club for those under 12—promises full or half days of beach adventures; an on-site golf course; and a full-service spa with such offerings as hydrotherapy massages, manicures, microdermabrasion and even teeth whitening. You have a choice of French, American or California cuisine. The St. Regis offers cooking & wine seminars on-site. Your dog gets bowls, a bed, bones and baggies. Plus, room service offers dog dishes—chicken or beef. $75 fee. 30-pound weight limit.

(714) - Costa Mesa

The Westin: South Coast Plaza

(714) 540-2500
686 Anton Blvd
(@ Bristol St)
Costa Mesa, California 92626
www.starwood.com/westin/southcoastplaza
Price Range: $$$

While the family is taking in Disneyland (it's a half-hour drive, traffic permitting) your dog can wait at the hotel. Just make sure you leave plenty of toys and arrange for a dog walker. Except for the Westin's signature Heavenly Dog Bed, the hotel offers no pet amenities or walking services. For exercise, a dog-friendly jogging trail is close by. If you prefer to relax, head to the spa or dine at the hotel's Mediterranean style restaurant, Pinot Provence. You may also enjoy the 400 shops at the high-end South Coast Plaza. No fee. 20-pound weight limit.

(760) - Palm Springs & Carlsbad

La Quinta Resort & Club

(800) 598-3828
49-499 Eisenhower Dr
(@ Washington St)
La Quinta, California 92253
www.laquintaresort.com
Price Range: $$$$$

Golf is the main draw for La Quinta: five world-class courses are within walking distance of the hotel. With fireplaces and mountain (or pool) views from the patios, the inviting rooms are easy to live in and difficult to leave. The spa and salon have some unusual offerings: Mustard Bath and the Celestial Shower treatments as well as Yamaguchi Feng-Shui haircuts and Tea Manicures. You can also play tennis at the top-rated La Quinta tennis club, or take a 20-minute drive to off-leash hiking trails. Dining options include several restaurants, which offer Mexican, seafood, steakhouse or spa cuisine. Guests with pups must book rooms with private patios. $100 fee. 30-pound weight limit.

The Westin: Mission Hills Resort

(760) 328-5955
71333 Dinah Shore Dr
(@ Bob Hope Dr)
Rancho Mirage, California 92270
www.starwood.com/westin/missionhills
Price Range: $$$$

Palm trees and waterfalls line the hotel's Moor-era Spanish buildings. This Westin boasts two world-class golf courses, three pools, a basketball court and a soccer field. The hotel's Bella Vista restaurant serves up Mediterranean cuisine, but the capper is Some Place Else, the Westin's own ice cream parlor. You're a quick drive from downtown Palm Springs, Agua Caliente Casino and the dog-friendly park at College of the Desert. The Westin will provide your dog with a bed and bowls. As long as she's leashed, your dog is welcome to join you on the hotel's gorgeous pathways. No fee. 40-pound weight limit.

Four Seasons Hotel: Aviara, North San Diego

(760) 603-6800
7100 Four Seasons Pt
(off Avaria Pkwy)
Carlsbad, California 92009
www.fourseasons.com/aviara
Price Range: $$$$$

This romantic Spanish Colonial oceanfront resort is nestled between a wildlife sanctuary and a golf course designed by Arnold Palmer. You can lounge in one of the poolside cabanas, play tennis or check out California Bistro, the resident French-California fusion restaurant. Spa aficionados may want to check out the Watsu massage—you get stretched and massaged while floating in a heated pool. Your pup will be pampered as well with freshly baked dog biscuits and his own Four Seasons bowls. Dogs are allowed to stay in the guestrooms unattended, as long as they are crated for housekeeping. No fee. 15-pound weight limit.

(858) - La Jolla & Rancho Santa Fe

La Valencia

(800) 451-0772
1132 Prospect St
(@ Herschel Ave)
La Jolla, California 92037
www.lavalencia.com

Price Range: $$$$

You'll know you're at a beachfront resort when you step in your room—the windows swing all the way open, allowing the soothing sound of the ocean and fresh salt-water air to waft into your room. Offerings include hot tubs, an outdoor heated pool, a fitness center, sauna, massages and facials. Award-winning tennis facilities are nearby, as is the Torrey Pines Golf Course, home of the Buick Invitational. There are three in-house restaurants, including the French-inspired Sky Room with a 180-degree ocean view. You can walk your pup through the upscale shopping district in La Jolla Village or jog with him along the Pacific. $75 per-night fee for each pet. 40-pound weight limit.

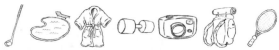

The Inn at Rancho Santa Fe

(800) 843-4661
5951 Linea Del Cielo (@ Lomas Santa Fe)
Rancho Santa Fe, California 92067
www.theinnatrsf.com/innrsf/intro.htm

Price Range: $$$

With Spanish-tiled roofs, private cottages and live music in the courtyard, the Inn is made for romance and relaxation. You can get a massage, play some tennis, take a weight-training class, play croquet on the front lawn or lounge in the pool. Book early to sample Southern California wine in the outdoor Dining Room. Trails and winding tree-lined roads offer dogs plenty of off-leash space and pups can swim at several dog-friendly beaches only five miles away. Theater buffs note: The Old Globe Theatres are nearby, as are award-winning wineries and the San Diego Zoo. $125 fee. 15-pound weight limit.

(619) - San Diego

W: San Diego

(619) 231-8220
421 West B St (@ State St)
San Diego, California 92101
www.starwood.com/whotels/sandiego

Price Range: $$$$

Swanky and a little quirky, this SoHo-chic W has a lot to offer. Comfy beds, window seats and splashes of color make the rooms a great place to hang out. Other perks include a fitness center with trainers, a steam room and an outdoor pool. There's a full menu of spa services—aromatherapy, massage, waxing and facials. For a true W experience, you can rent one of the three cabanas on the rooftop, and enjoy global cuisine in the heated sand by the fire pit. Dog amenities include a toy, treats, tags, baggies, beds, bowls and any pet-care referrals you might need. $25 per pet per night, $100 fee. No weight limit.

The Westin: Horton Plaza
(619) 239-2200
910 Broadway Cir
(off Broadway)
San Diego, California 92101
www.starwood.com/westin/hortonplaza
Price Range: $$$
This Westin is adjacent to Horton Plaza Mall, which offers more than 130 shops, and four blocks from the dog-friendly, tree-lined Gaslamp District. This quaint neighborhood offers live entertainment, funky restaurants and eclectic boutiques. You're also close to the city's oldest park: Pantoja is a pleasant patch of greenery squeezed into San Diego's revamped downtown area. If your pet needs to make a pit stop while at the hotel, there's a grassy area behind the Federal Building. The hotel provides your pup a Westin Heavenly Dog Bed, bowls and treats. People perks include in-room spa services, manicures, pedicures, massage and Pilates. No fee. 40-pound weight limit.

(805) - Santa Barbara

Four Seasons Resort: Santa Barbara
(805) 969-2261
1260 Channel Dr
(between Butterfly Ln & Bonnymede Dr)
Santa Barbara, California 93108
www.fourseasons.com/santabarbara
Price Range: $$$$$
This exquisite, Spanish Colonial Four Seasons, overlooking the Pacific Ocean, is situated in Santa Barbara's posh Montecito area. Activities include tennis, lounging poolside, spa treatments and golf. Children-specific activities as well as special

amenities keep kids happy. The hotel boasts the Marina and the Patio restaurants and La Salsa lounge. Guests with pets are booked in one of 12 cottages, that come with a living room, patio furniture, fireplace and a private entrance. Pups will be treated to toys and bones, plus trips to the nearby pet-friendly beach. Dogs are not allowed to stay in the room unattended, so take your dog with you or ask the hotel to schedule a pet-sitter. No fee. 50-pound weight limit.

San Ysidro Ranch
(800) 368-6788
900 San Ysidro Ln
(@ El Bosque Rd)
Santa Barbara, California 93108
www.sanysidroranch.com
Price Range: $$$$

Declared one of the 10 Most Romantic Destinations in the World by the Travel Channel, San Ysidro is a regular on the *Condé Nast* Gold List and *Travel & Leisure's* 500 Greatest Hotels in the World list. This idyllic Relais & Chateaux hotel—nestled in the foothills of the stunning Santa Ynez Mountains—was the fairy-tale setting for Vivien Leigh and Sir Laurence Olivier's wedding as well as John and Jackie Kennedy's honeymoon. Endless accolades have been bestowed on the hotel's restaurants. Dogs are allowed in the cottage-style rooms of this luxe hideaway, which offers 17 miles of dog-friendly hiking trails on the property and lush gardens. $100 fee.

Colorado

(970) - Ski Towns

Hotel Jerome
Sky Hotel
St. Regis: Aspen
Elk Mountain Resort
Hotel Telluride
The Lodge at Vail

(303) - Denver & Westminster

Brown Palace Hotel
Hotel Monaco: Denver
Hotel Teatro
The Westin: Tabor Center
The Westin: Westminster

(970) - Ski Towns

Elk Mountain Resort
(970) 252-4900
97 Elk Walk
(between Dave Wood Rd & Elk Walk)
Montrose, Colorado 81401
www.slh.com/elkmountain
Price Range: $$$$$
This rustic, luxe resort earns top marks for creating an eco-friendly sporting paradise amid the breathtaking Colorado Rockies. Outdoor activities include hunting, rock climbing, hiking and horseback riding, as well as winter skiing for both experts and beginners. Their family-friendly philosophy, which includes pets, is exceptional. Dogs are allowed throughout the property and in all the buildings, with the exception of the restaurants. Complimentary dog offerings include a comfy wool bed, porcelain dishes, a bag of toys and plenty of treats.

Hotel Jerome

(800) 331-7213
3310 E Main St
(between N Spring & Original sts)
Aspen, Colorado 81611
www.hoteljerome.com

Price Range: $$$$

Both *Travel & Leisure* and *Condé Nast Traveler* have given high marks to this landmark hotel, which recently underwent a $7 million renovation while preserving many of its Victorian touches. Dogs are treated to a complimentary J-Bone from the pastry chef, and the hotel will arrange for pet-sitting while you are out. Dog-friendly Aspen makes it easy for your pup to tag along. Dogs are welcome in most of the nearby shops, and city parks and hiking trails are within walking distance of the hotel. The Jerome encourages leashes but don't be surprised if you happen upon a Great Pyrenees, a frequent hotel guest, lounging on the sofa. $75 fee. No weight limit.

Hotel Telluride

(970) 369-1188
199 N Cornet St
(@ Colorado Ave)
Telluride, Colorado 81435
www.slh.com/telluride

Price Range: $$$

This picture-perfect 3-year-old lodge boasts fireplaces and views of the 14,000-foot San Juan peaks. The mountain-chic hotel features plush, Ralph Lauren-style furnishings and a host of outdoor activities, including fishing, skiing and horseback riding. Your pup's picture is taken at arrival and placed in their photo album of pet guests. Dog amenities include complimentary bones and treats at check-in, as well as a featherbed for your pet. You can schedule dog walking, or book your pup a tour of the quaint town of Telluride and a walk in the mountains. But plan ahead: Pet rooms are limited. $25 per day. 80-pound weight limit.

The Lodge at Vail

(800) 231-0136
174 East Gore Creek Dr
(between Willow Bridge Rd & Bridge St)
Vail, Colorado 81657
www.lodgeatvail.rockresorts.com

Price Range: $$$$

Skiers will love this slope-side lodge in the heart of Vail
Village. If you're stiff after a day on the slopes, rest in the hotel
hot tub or take a dip in the heated outdoor pool. People rave
about the food at the Wildflower, and Mickey's Piano Bar is a
favorite with both tourists and locals. If you're seeking solitude,
check into the Lodge's outpost—Game Creek Chalet. Located
in Game Creek Bowl, it comes with a personal chef and ski
instructor. Dogs are welcome, but the Lodge doesn't offer pet
amenities. However, if you're out for the day, they will handle
dog-walking duties. $25 per night. No weight limit.

St. Regis: Aspen

(888) 454-9005
315 E Dean St
(@ S Monarch St)
Aspen, Colorado 81611
www.stregisaspen.com

Price Range: $$$$$

Where the rich go to relax, Aspen caters to dogs in the same
fashion as they cater to the stars. The luxurious St. Regis hotel,
welcoming dogs of all sizes, is no exception. For a $100 all-
inclusive fee, your pup will get dog bowls, dishes, bedding
and gourmet dog biscuits. The concierge will provide a list of
potential adventures for you and your dog and arrange for
pet-sitting services for the few times when your dog isn't welcome. Those who wish to take advantage of the stellar shopping will be pleased to know that dogs are welcome in many
of the stores.

Sky Hotel

(800) 882-2582
709 E Durant Ave (@ S Spring St)
Aspen, Colorado 81611
www.theskyhotel.com

Price Range: $$$$$

Kimpton has done it again: this uber-hip art deco-gone-moun-
tain rustic hotel—sedate by Kimpton standards—offers luxe
accommodations. Imagine fabulous faux-fur throws strewn
across plush ivory bed linens. Perks include a ski-in location;
a pool, complete with outdoor fireplace; complimentary
evening wine hour; a 24-hour fitness center, wireless Internet
access; and a fireplace in the suites. The hotel's 39 Degrees
Lounge is a local and tourist hot spot. Dogs stay free, but
spring for the It's a Dog's Life package, and your pup gets a
bed, treats, a $50 gift certificate to a pet boutique and a map
of dog-friendly hiking trails. Dog walking and pet-sitting can
be arranged through the hotel. No weight limit.

(303) - Denver, Westminster

Brown Palace Hotel

(800) 321-2599
321 17th St (@ Tremont Pl)
Denver, Colorado 80202
www.brownpalace.com

Price Range: $$$$

The historic Brown Palace treats dogs like kings offering
amenities, such as a bed, food and water bowls, treats, a dog
room-service menu and the option of booking the in-house
dog walker. The hotel's comfy rooms are laid out around a
seven-story atrium where high tea is an elegant afternoon ritu-
al. You're also close to all kinds of shopping in downtown
Denver, including the outdoor, dog-friendly 16th Street mall.
Important: You are required to show your dog's papers to
prove your pup's vaccinations are up to date. $50 fee. 25-
pound weight limit.

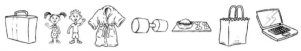

Hotel Monaco: Denver

(800) 990-1303
1717 Champa St
(between 17th & 18th sts)
Denver, Colorado 80202
www.monaco-denver.com

Price Range: $$$

A *Travel & Leisure* Top 500 Hotels in the World pick, the Hotel
Monaco was also *T & L's* pick for the Best Business Hotel in
Denver. Plush room options in this fabulously funky hotel
include the Miles Davis, John Lennon, Grace Slick (Jefferson
Airplane) and Monte Carlo suites. Standard dog amenities
include a bed, bowls, treats and a dog-park map. The
concierge will arrange dog-care services, including dog walk-
ing, pet sitting, grooming and massage. Hotel perks include
complimentary evening wine hour and an on-site Aveda spa. If
you're traveling sans dog, the hotel will loan you a goldfish to
keep you company during your stay. No fee. No weight limit.

Hotel Teatro

(303) 228-1100
1100 14th St (@ Lawrence St)
Denver, Colorado 80202
www.slh.com/teatro

Price Range: $$$$

A Small Luxury Hotels of the World member, the Hotel Teatro
dates back to 1911—but dog perks are something new. The
Canine Companion Program begins with Fiji water on ice and
also includes dog massage, a full dog menu, a personalized
dog tag as well as bowls, a bed, toys and treats. Dog walking
and day care are available at no additional charge. Located
across from the Denver Centre for the Performing Arts, the ele-
gant decor incorporates costumes from past productions.
Guest rooms provide high-tech business amenities, including a
laser printer, scanner, fax and high-speed Internet access. Be
sure to check out both of their award-winning restaurants. No
fee. No weight limit.

The Westin: Tabor Center

(303) 572-9100
1672 Lawrence St
(between 16th & 17th sts)
Denver, Colorado 80202
www.starwood.com/westin/taborcenter

Price Range: $$$

This elegant business hotel in Denver does a great job of blending style with function. High-speed Internet and state-of-the-art fitness equipment are offered alongside the comfort of the Westin's signature Heavenly Bed and ergonomic chairs. The indoor/outdoor mile-high pool offers an amazing view of the Rockies. You also have access to the sauna, whirlpools and racquetball courts. Check out V's Martini Bar for cocktails; the Palm for steak and seafood; and the acclaimed Augusta for breakfast. Your pup will get a bed and bowls at check in. Skyline Park, just behind the hotel, is a great place to walk your dog. No fee. 30-pound weight limit.

The Westin: Westminster

(303) 410-5000
10600 Westminster Blvd
(between Highway 36 & 104th Ave)
Westminster, Colorado 80020
www.starwood.com/westin/westminster

Price Range: $$$

To reach this mountain Westin, you'll cross a charming foot-bridge that offers views of cascading waterfalls and lofty mountain peaks. Located halfway between Colorado's sister cities, Boulder and Denver, the hotel is close to boutique shopping, local theater and fine dining. Take your pup along, and he'll enjoy the spacious, dog-friendly park out back. At night, your pup can cozy up in a Westin dog bed. The hotel asks that you crate your pup while you're out. No weight limit.

Connecticut

(203) – Greenwich & Stamford

Delamar Greenwich Harbor
The Westin: Stamford

Delamar Greenwich Harbor

(203) 661-9800
500 Steamboat Rd
(off Interstate 95)
Greenwich, Connecticut 06830
www.slh.com/delamar
Price Range: $$$$$

This classic Connecticut hotel, a member of the Small Leading
Hotels of the World, offers harbor views and a 600-square-foot
private dock. Polo, boating and riding are all on the menu,
though you may be content to shop your way through
Greenwich. Birds, cats and fish are welcome here, and dogs
receive a personalized name tag, food and water dishes, a
bone and a bed. The hotel will coordinate walking, day-care
and spa treatments for your pup through outside providers.
Small dogs only. $25 daily fee.

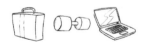

The Westin: Stamford

(203) 967-2222
1 Stamford Pl
(between Fairfield & Greenwich aves)
Stamford, Connecticut 06902
www.starwood.com/westin/stamford
Price Range: $$$

Classic with subtle eastern influences, this Westin is made for
the business traveler. Strategically located near Manhattan,
Westchester, JFK and La Guardia, the Westin Stamford offers

high-speed Internet access as well as a business center. Other perks include the 24-hour fitness center and Area, the in-house American restaurant. Your pup will receive bowls and a signature Heavenly Dog Bed at check-in. The hotel is in close proximity to 83-acres of waterside walking trails at Cove Island Park, on Long Beach Sound. $25 daily fee. 30-pound weight limit.

Delaware

(302) – Wilmington

Hotel DuPont

Hotel DuPont
(800) 441-9019
1007 N Market St
(@ 11th St)
Wilmington, Delaware 19801
www.dupont.com/hotel
Price Range: $$$$$
Built in 1913 by French and Italian craftsmen, the DuPont now features refurbished rooms with brass-fitted baths. In fact, the hotel recently received the prestigious Gold Key Award for Best Guest Room Design in the World. Dogs are welcome. However, the DuPont doesn't provide any pet amenities. People perks include the nearby DuPont Country Club's tennis courts and an 18-hole championship golf course, home to the LPGA Championship. You're also close to the Brandywine Valley as well as museums, gardens and art galleries. $100 fee. 25-pound weight limit.

District of Columbia

(202) – Washington

Four Seasons Hotel: Washington, D.C.
Hay-Adams Hotel
The Hotel George
Hotel Helix
Hotel Madera
Hotel Monaco: Washington, D.C.
Hotel Rouge
Jefferson Hotel D.C.
The Madison D.C.
Mandarin Oriental: Washington, D.C.
The Ritz-Carlton: Georgetown
The Ritz-Carlton: Washington, D.C.
Sofitel: Lafayette Square
St. Regis: Washington, D.C.
Tabard Inn
Topaz Hotel
The Westin: Embassy Row
The Westin: Grand
Willard InterContinental

(202) – Washington, D.C.

Four Seasons Hotel: Washington, D.C.
(202) 342-0444
2800 NW Pennsylvania Ave (@ 28th St)
Washington, District of Columbia 20007
www.fourseasons.com/washington
Price Range: $$$$$
Located at the corner of M Street and Pennsylvania Avenue in historic Georgetown, this Four Seasons exudes a timeless elegance and a sense of tradition. You'll have views of monu-

ments from your balcony. And the White House, Arlington National Cemetery and the Library of Congress are only minutes away. The three-story fitness club offers yoga, spinning and weight training, and you can swim laps beneath a skylight. Massages and body polishes are available at the posh spa. The hotel restaurant, Seasons, offers a daily tasting menu, and afternoon tea is served in the Garden Terrace. Your pup gets freshly baked dog biscuits, bowls and a bed. No fee. 15-pound weight limit.

Hay-Adams Hotel
(800) 853-6807
800 NW 16th St
(@ H St)
Washington, District of Columbia   20006
www.hayadams.com
Price Range: $$$$$
This residential D.C. hotel dates back to the 1920s, and the pillars and groomed gardens mimic those of the White House. Fitting, since the hotel sits across the street from the president's place, making for a unique dog-walking experience. Other city landmarks within walking distance, include the Smithsonian, the Washington Monument and the Mall. The Hay-Adams offers family-friendly events, including high tea for children with Woodrow the White House Mouse. For a more serious meal, try Sunday brunch at the hotel's Lafayette Room. There is a 20-pound weight limit for pets and no fee charged unless damage occurs.

The Hotel George
(800) 576-8331
15 E St
(between New Jersey Ave & Capitol St)
Washington, District of Columbia   20001
www.hotelgeorge.com
Price Range: $$$$

The dollar bill has become pop art at this uber-hip, four-star D.C. hotel. Unlike most hotels, where the comfort level seems to be inversely proportional to the hipster quotient, this luxe, comfy hotel has it all. Not a surprise, given that George is a member of the standout Kimpton Hotel Group. Dogs get a goodie bag at check-in, which includes food bowls, treats, a guide to pet-friendly parks and sights, and a Pet Session in Progress door hanger. Buy the My Dog Gets Presidential Treatment at the George package and go sightseeing while your dog enjoys an aromatherapy bath and massage at the Wagtime Pet Spa and Boutique. No fee. No weight limit.

Hotel Helix
(800) 706-1202
1430 NW Rhode Island Ave
(between 14th & 15th sts)
Washington, District of Columbia 20006
www.hotelhelix.com
Price Range: $$$
The sky-blue eleven-foot-high lawn chairs at the entrance beckon travelers to this electric-colored, Warhol-inspired boutique hotel. Specialty suites include Zone (all about bliss), Eats (think munchies) and Bunk (perfect for kids) rooms. One of the wackier members of the Kimpton Hotel Group, Helix offers the same level of outstanding service for dogs that they offer people. A gift bag for your pup includes food bowls, cleanup bags, treats and for you, dog-bone shaped playing cards. The hotel will also provide you with a map of places to walk your dog as well as dog salons in the area. No fee. No weight limit.

Hotel Madera
(800) 430-1202
1310 NW New Hampshire Ave
(between N & 20th sts)
Washington, District of Columbia 20036
www.hotelmadera.com

Price Range: $$$

This Dupont Circle Kimpton hotel offers a tranquil retreat in the heart of D.C. You're still within walking distance of the Mall and the White House, and you're not too far from the rest of D.C.'s cultural offerings. Room options include the Cardio Room, with a treadmill or bike; Nosh Room, with kitchenette and grocery-delivery service; Flash Room with a computer and Internet access; and the Screening Room, with a DVD player and library. The hotel keeps a water bowl at the entrance to the hotel for their dog guests. Dogs receive welcome treats and the hotel staff will fetch anything you forgot—they call it personal pet shopping. No fee. No weight limit.

Hotel Monaco: Washington, D.C.

(800) 649-1202
700 F St (@ 7th St)
Washington, District of Columbia 20004
www.monaco-dc.com

Price Range: $$$

Located inside the historic 1839 Tariff Building—the first marble building in D.C.—the Hotel Monaco is magnificent. Vaulted ceilings, with exquisite crown mouldings, combined with plush, timeless furniture make this the grandest of the boutique Kimpton hotels. The hotel, which opened in 2002, made the *Condé Nast* 80 Best New Hotels in the World list. Guest perks include a complimentary evening wine hour; a 24-hour fitness center; access to the YMCA pool; and designated tall rooms with longer beds and raised shower heads. Dog amenities include bowls, dog treats, a walking map and a list of area dog resources. Additionally, the concierge will arrange for pet sitting or dog walking, and room service offers meals especially for your dog. No fee. No weight limit.

Hotel Rouge

(800) 738-1202
1315 NW 16th Street (@ Rhode Island Ave)

Washington, District of Columbia 20036
www.rougehotel.com

Price Range: $$$

This high-tech, luxury boutique hotel near the downtown D.C. business district caters to movers and shakers and the dogs that love them. Unabashedly targeting a younger, wireless crowd, the hotel offers 15 specialty rooms—including Chat, Chill and Chow—in addition to its regular rooms. Upgrade to the No Need to Beg package, and the hotel will provide your pet with a fire-hydrant placemat, bowls, liver biscotti, clean-up bags and a deluxe room. If you stay on a weekend, check out the last-call Bloody Mary and cold-pizza hour. No fee. No weight limit.

Jefferson Hotel D.C.

(202) 347-2200
1200 16th St NW (@ M St)
Washington, District of Columbia 20036
www.thejeffersondc.com

Price Range: $$$$$

Would you like room service for your dog? At the Jefferson, it's all part of a pet-friendly philosophy that includes complimentary water bowls, dishes, meals and menus. Along with one free daily meal delivery, the hotel provides dog biscuits at the mini-bar and a sightseeing map that includes the White House only four blocks away. Your dog is also welcome to stroll through the Jefferson's lobby, alongside visiting dignitaries and heads of state while you view letters and documents signed by (who else?) Thomas Jefferson. No fee. No weight limit.

The Madison D.C.

(800) 424-8577
1177 NW 15th St (@ M & 15th sts)
Washington, District of Columbia 20005
www.themadisondc.com

Price Range: $$$$$

White gloved and conservatively dressed, the Madison's staff strives to provide genteel and anticipatory service for all their guests. The rooms are decorated in an early 18th-century style, upgraded with modern amenities. Perks include a fitness center, a sauna, a steam room, massages and manicures. The Federalist—a power breakfast hot spot—serves hearty fare, and Postscript, the resident bar frequented by all the good old boys, is appropriately furnished in Mahogany. Your pup will get the royal treatment: The hotel provides meals, treats, beds, bowls, walking and pet-sitting services. Also close by is dog-friendly Fort DuPont Park. No fee. No weight limit.

Mandarin Oriental: Washington, D.C.

(888) 888-1778
1330 SW Maryland Ave
(between 14th & Elliot sts)
Washington, District of Columbia 20024
www.mandarinoriental.com/hotel/535000001.asp
Price Range: $$$$$
The D.C. outpost of this exquisitely Eastern five-star chain, a favorite of renowned architect I.M. Pei, does not disappoint. The elegantly appointed, feng shui-inspired design offers guests a level of tranquility only attained in the finest Asian hotels. Although the staff requests your pup stay leashed while on hotel property, dogs can play off-leash at the 5,000-square-foot park across the street or along the waterfront. The hotel, which is still revising their pet policy, currently offers pet beds, bowls and snacks at check-in. No fee. 40-pound weight limit.

The Ritz-Carlton: Georgetown

(202) 912-4100
3100 NW South St
(@ M St & Wisconsin Ave)
Washington, District of Columbia 20007
www.ritzcarlton.com/hotels/georgetown
Price Range: $$$$$

The historic Georgetown incinerator building has been transformed into a contemporary Ritz. The hotel does capitalize on its history, particularly with the Fahrenheit restaurant and Degrees lounge—the site of a monthly Mutt-ini Hour. This happy hour for people and their pups features everything from gourmet treats to dog massage therapy. Dog beds and bowls are available, and for active dogs, a walking trail begins just outside the hotel and stretches all the way to the Lincoln Memorial, Washington Monument and back—a minimum two-hour jaunt. $125 fee. 50-pound weight limit.

The Ritz-Carlton: Washington, D.C.

(202) 835-0500
1150 NW 22nd St (between M St & 22nd St)
Washington, District of Columbia 20037
www.ritzcarlton.com/hotels/washington_dc
Price Range: $$$$$

This posh West End Ritz made the *Condé Nast Traveler*'s Gold List. While it doesn't offer the spa or fitness facilities found at many other Ritz-Carltons, this hotel does provide the gourmet Grill restaurant with an exhibition kitchen, and the largest ballroom in the city. Swanky Georgetown shopping is just around the corner and you're a 10-minute drive away from the White House and monuments. The hotel will arrange dog-walking service, but if you ask, a staff member will usually volunteer to take your dog on a quick walk. Dog bowls and treats are available on request. $125 fee with a two-pet maximum. 25-pound weight limit.

St. Regis: Washington, D.C.

(202) 638-2626
923 16th St (@ K St)
Washington, District of Columbia 20006
www.starwood.com/stregis/washingtondc
Price Range: $$$$$

This elegant, Italian Renaissance-style St. Regis has housed royalty, prime ministers and every U.S. president since Calvin Coolidge. Given top honors by *Condé Nast* and *Travel & Leisure*, this antique-adorned hotel, lit by chandeliers, also accommodates dogs. Your pup will receive a bed and bowls at check-in, along with any referrals you might need. People offerings include a 24-hour fitness center and a business center as well as high-speed Internet and flat-screen TVs. The St. Regis restaurant serves American cuisine. Be sure to bring appropriate attire: The dress code is enforced. No fee. 25-pound weight limit.

Sofitel: Lafayette Square
(202) 730-8800
806 NW 15th St
(between Lafayette Sq & the White House)
Washington, District of Columbia 20005
www.sofitel.com
Price Range: $$$
Built in the late 1800s, the Sofitel Lafayette Square mixes traditional design with contemporary pieces. The rooms are done in simple lines and cozy fabrics, darker woods with bold splashes of color. There's both a business and a fitness center within the hotel, as well as high-speed Internet access. Café 15 serves French cuisine and if you're visiting in the warmer months you can enjoy your meal on the terrace. If you give the concierge advance notice, the hotel creates a custom-designed welcome basket for your pup. McPherson Square Park and Lafayette Square Park are right outside your door, as is the White House. No fee. No weight limit.

Tabard Inn
(202) 785-1277
1739 N St (between 17th & 18th sts)
Washington, District of Columbia 20036
www.tabardinn.com
Price Range: $$$

Dogs are welcome at this intimate 40-room hotel, but pet services are limited. While your dog can't be left alone in the room, the hotel staff will point you to a highly recommended dog day-care facility a block away. This Victorian hotel has all kinds of unique nooks and crannies as well as two rooms fit for business conferences. You and your dog will get plenty of exercise during your stay: The four-story Tabard Inn, which maintains much of its original structure, has no elevator. $20 daily fee per pet. No weight limit.

Topaz Hotel
(800) 775-1202
1733 N St (between 17th & 18th sts)
Washington, District of Columbia 20036
www.topazhotel.com
Price Range: $$$$

Self-proclaimed as "D.C.'s most enlightened boutique hotel," the Topaz lives up to its name by offering Namastay Rooms, daily horoscopes and energy drinks. The decor—very *Willy Wonka and the Chocolate Factory*—creates an environment that is as whimsical as it is comfortable. Aspiring yogis may want to stay over the weekend when the Doga package is available. It includes a free yoga basket with a mat for you to use while watching the hotel's in-house yoga channel. You aren't the only one who will be doing downward dog—dogs get their own yoga mat and a copy of the book "Doga for Dogs." Dog walking can be arranged through the hotel. No fee. No weight limit.

The Westin: Embassy Row
(202) 293-2100
2100 NW Massachusetts Ave
(@ 21st & Massachusetts sts)
Washington, District of Columbia 20008
www.starwood.com/westin
Price Range: $$$

The Westin Embassy Row looks more like a southern mansion than a link in a high-end corporate hotel chain. The elegant rooms are furnished with turn of the century accents, and all include the signature Heavenly Bed. The hotel offers high-speed Internet as well as a fitness center. The Fairfax Room serves eclectic cuisine—venture out if you want a specific genre of food. The location makes touring D.C. easy—Capitol Hill, the Washington Monument, the Vietnam Memorial and the Smithsonian Institute are less than a mile away. Your pup will receive treats, toys and a bed at check-in. The always-busy Dupont Circle—a dog-walking hot spot—is a short walk away. No fee. No weight limit.

The Westin: Grand
(202) 429-0100
2350 M St
(@ 24th St)
Washington, District of Columbia 20037
www.starwood.com/westin/washingtondc
Price Range: $$$
Grand is the operative word at this stunning D.C. luxury hotel perfectly positioned in Foggy Bottom. Georgetown, the monuments, the Mall and the White House are all within walking distance. If your dog needs more exercise than your site-seeing tour affords, walk him on a nearby trail or head to Rock Creek National Park seven blocks away. If you need a workout, visit the on-site fitness center with flat-screen TVs at each machine or take a dip in the enormous outdoor pool. The Westin provides your pup with its signature Heavenly Dog Bed. $50 deposit. 40-pound weight limit.

Willard InterContinental
(202) 628-9100
1401 NW Pennsylvania Ave (@ 14th St)
Washington, District of Columbia 20004
www.washington.intercontinental.com

Price Range: $$$$$

This historic hotel calls itself the crown jewel of Pennsylvania Avenue, which is saying quite a bit considering the White House is two blocks down the street. *Travel & Leisure's* 2003 pick for the Best Business Hotel in Washington. The Willard—with a traditional, Federal-style design—has been hosting the rich and famous since 1850 and treats dogs like traveling dignitaries. Pup offerings include meals, treats and bowls, along with dog-walking and pet-sitting services. Your dog is allowed in the room alone, but let the front desk know so they can warn housekeeping. No fee. No weight limit.

Florida

(954) – Fort Lauderdale

The Westin: Fort Lauderdale

(305) – Miami

The Ritz-Carlton: Coconut Grove
Four Seasons Hotel: Miami
Mandarin Oriental: Miami
Mayfair House Hotel
Sofitel: Miami
Eden Roc Resort and Spa
Shore Club
The Tides Hotel

(786) – Miami Beach

The Ritz-Carlton: South Beach

(407) – Orlando

Walt Disney World Swan
Loews: Hard Rock Hotel
Westin Grand Bohemian Orlando

(561) – Palm Beach & Manalapan

The Ritz-Carlton: Palm Beach
Brazilian Court
Chesterfield Hotel
Four Seasons Resort: Palm Beach

(727) – Palm Harbor

The Westin: Innisbrook Golf Resort

(941) – Sarasota

The Ritz Carlton: Sarasota

(954) - Fort Lauderdale

The Westin: Fort Lauderdale
(954) 772-1331
400 Corporate Dr
(@ Cypress Creek & NE 7th Ave)
Fort Lauderdale, Florida 33334
www.starwood.com/westin/fortlauderdale
Price Range: $$$

This Fort Lauderdale hotel offers indoor and outdoor conference space as well as a pool and access to beaches. So be sure to pack sunblock and swimwear along with your power suit. The hotel provides dogs with a welcome package that includes a Heavenly Dog Bed, bowl, baggie and a list of dog-friendly beaches. You can also leash up your pup and go for a jog on the mile-and-a-half trail that runs right behind the Westin. People perks include a fitness center near the three-acre lagoon, a dry sauna and fresh pasta at Alfiere's Mediterranean Bistro. $50 deposit. 40-pound weight limit.

(305) - Miami

Eden Roc Resort and Spa
(800) 327-8337
4525 Collins Ave
(@ Bayview Dr)
Miami Beach, Florida 33140
www.edenrocresort.com
Price Range: $$$

This magnificent, Renaissance-style resort offers guests a piece of paradise. The resort spa, one of the country's best, provides a range of body treatments as well as floor-to-ceiling windows overlooking the Atlantic. The fitness center offers the same ocean view, and workouts include daily yoga and spinning classes. The Eden Roc also hosts two pools facing Miami Beach and several water activities, including, parasailing and a scuba certification class for beginners. While the resort doesn't provide any dog amenities, nearby South Beach is full of upscale boutiques—where dogs are welcome and sometimes treated better than people. No fee. 15-pound weight limit.

Four Seasons Hotel: Miami
(305) 358-3535
1435 Brickell Ave
(between 14th Ter & 14th Ln)
Miami, Florida 33131
www.fourseasons.com/miami
Price Range: $$$$$

Tropical with geometric accents, the Four Seasons captures the essence of Miami without falling into the 1980s faux-glamour trap. The beach is only minutes away, but before hitting the sand, you might check out the three spectacular hotel pools. The main pool offers cabanas and pool attendants, another pool is exclusively for children under 12, and the Palm Grove Pool is shallow enough for a lounge chair. The Splash Spa offers massage and skin-care treatments. Other hotel perks include a fitness center, golf and tennis. The hotel restaurant, Acqua, serves Italian fare. You can eat poolside at Bahia, often accompanied by live music. Your pup gets treats, bowls and a bed. No fee. 15-pound weight limit.

Mandarin Oriental: Miami
(305) 913-8288
500 Brickell Key Dr
(@ Brickell Ave)
Miami, Florida 33131
www.mandarin-oriental.com
Price Range: $$$$$

The Far East meets Miami glamour at this Mandarin Oriental. Voted Best Spa in the US by *Travel & Leisure*, AAA five-diamond rated and located prominently beachside, there is little this hotel doesn't offer. The suites are gorgeously detailed with Asian decor, tropical flowers and Spanish marble. There's an infinity pool, a full fitness center and a private beach. Golf and tennis are close by. Yoga and Pilates classes are taught on-site. Azul, the award-winning Asian-Latin restaurant sits alongside the M Bar, which features 250 types of martinis. Your pup is provided with bedding and treats. A 10-minute drive will take you to dog-friendly Key Biscayne. $200 fee, $100 of which is refundable. 40-pound weight limit.

Mayfair House Hotel

(800) 433-4555
3000 Florida Ave
(@ Virginia St)
Miami, Florida 33133
www.mayfairhousehotel.com

Price Range: $$$

This Coconut Grove hotel has plenty of awards adorning the walls, including the Mobil four-star and AAA four-diamond awards. The suites were renovated in 2003—be prepared for loud bursts of color and unusual fabrics, e.g., vinyl. Each room has their own terrace and either a Roman or Japanese soaking tub. The airport, Miami Beach and downtown are about 10 miles away. If you are in the mood for new shoes or a movie, just step outside: the Mayfair sits inside a shopping and entertainment village. Your dog is welcome, but it will cost you: $200 deposit, plus a $20 daily fee. 35-pound weight limit.

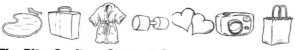

The Ritz-Carlton: Coconut Grove

(305) 644-4680
3300 SW 27th Ave
(between S Bayshore Dr & Tigertail Ave)
Coconut Grove, Florida 33133
www.ritzcarlton.com/hotels/coconut_grove

Price Range: $$$$$

Funky, zany, bohemian—that's Coconut Grove, the avant-garde village surrounding the Ritz-Carlton. Check out the hotel's decadent Sunday brunch, with everything from lobster to lamb chops, plus a spectacular view of the courtyard waterfall. The hotel has no formal dog amenities, but plenty of dog-friendly places are nearby, including CocoWalk, the open-air shopping area and Key Biscayne, plus two state parks are just across the Rickenbacker Causeway. $125 fee. No weight limit.

Shore Club
(305) 695-3100
1901 Collins Ave
(@ 19th St)
Miami Beach, Florida 33139
www.shoreclub.com
Price Range: $$$$$
Clean modern lines meet Middle Eastern influences at this spectacular hotel in South Beach. From the lantern-lit lobby through the pillow strewn Redroom bar to the cabanas by the glassy pools, the Shore Club knows how to make an impression. You can get lost in the secret passageways of the gardens, pick up the latest in fashion at Scoop, or get a new style at Pipino Salon—all in house. Nobu dishes out renowned Japanese cuisine, and Ago serves Tuscan fare on the Ocean Front Terrace. The full spa menu includes massages, facials, waxing and mani-pedis. FYI—no dogs on the beach. $100 fee. 50-pound weight limit.

Sofitel: Miami
(305) 264-4888
5800 Blue Lagoon Dr
(off N Red Rd)
Miami, Florida 33126
www.sofitel.com
Price Range: $$$$$
With an energetic staff, a lively atmosphere and fashionistas strutting the grounds, this Sofitel is the epitome of hip. Rooms

feature mod decor, plenty of space and fluffy comforters. If you're looking for a place to walk your dog, there's a gigantic park outside where he can run free, with plenty of water available. If you want to treat your pet to some spa time, head for the nearby Chez Puchy Pet Grooming. $50 fee. Somewhat flexible 20-pound weight limit.

The Tides Hotel
(866) 438-4337
1220 Ocean Dr (@ 12th St)
Miami Beach, Florida 33139
www.thetideshotel.com
Price Range: $$$$$
The ultimate in laidback luxury, this art-deco hotel promises pristine but plush accommodations and superb service. Amenities include poolside wireless Internet access, Aveda bath products, robes, and the topper: slippers. The hotel sits within walking distance of Miami's nightlife, shopping, dining, convention center, museums and theaters. The beach is just steps away, where the hotel will have chairs and umbrellas waiting for you. The hotel's softer qualities make for a quieter Miami experience, while its more risqué qualities, like the topless pool, keep it interesting. Dogs are welcome but the amenities are up to you. $100 fee. 20-pound weight limit.

(786) - Miami Beach

The Ritz-Carlton: South Beach
(786) 276-4000
1 Lincoln Rd
(@ Collins Ave)
Miami, Florida 33139

www.ritzcarlton.com/resorts/south_beach
Price Range: $$$$$
On fashionable Lincoln Road, where this Ritz sits, everyone
seems to have a dog. The hotel staff will arrange any services
your pet might need and take care of dog-walking duties. The
Miami Ritz-Carlton, recently restored to its original 1953 art-
deco design, boasts a $2 million art collection. This Ritz also
offers supervised kids activities on Miami Beach and a Saks
Fifth Avenue Wedding Dress Shopping package—which also
includes spa treatments. If you'd rather sun, the hotel has
poolside tanning butlers standing by with sunblock. The one
negative: No pets on the beach, period. And police are quick
to ticket. $250 fee. 35-pound weight limit.

(407) - Orlando

Loews: Hard Rock Hotel
(407) 503-7625
5800 Universal Blvd
(@ Vineland Rd)
Orlando, Florida 32819
www.loewshotels.com/hotels/orlando_hard_rock/default.asp
Price Range: $$$$
The Hard Rock offers a lot more than loud rock music. This
enormous hotel wraps around a 150-foot pool, and the guest
rooms offer a contemporary design. Kids' suites are fitted with
play areas, and the Graceland suite even includes a grand
piano. The hotel sits near Orlando's shopping and nightlife, as
well as Universal Studios and Sea World. Dogs receive rock-
star treatment, with a mat, bowl, treats and a Do Not Disturb
sign. The concierge will arrange for pet services, including
dog-walking or sitting. Unless you're up for a 15-minute drive
to the closest off-leash dog park, your pup will have to get by
with on-leash entertainment. No fee. No weight limit.

Walt Disney World Swan

(888) 828-8850
1500 Epcot Resorts Blvd
Lake Buena Vista, Florida 32830
www.swandolphin.com

Price Range: $$$$

Located inside the Disney resort, the Swan hotel offers transportation to all Disney World parks and attractions, priority seating at Disney restaurants and the option to chow down with Disney characters. There are several swimming pools to cool off in after a day at the theme parks, and tennis courts and golf courses are nearby. By Disney decree, dogs are banished to the kennels at Epcot Center, where amenities consist of food, water and brief, daily walks. You can visit at any time: In fact, the staff prefers that owners come by at least once a day. There is a $9 per day fee, a $2.50 fee per walk. No weight limit.

Westin Grand Bohemian Orlando

(407) 313-9000
325 S Orange Ave
(@ Jackson St)
Orlando, Florida 32801
www.starwood.com/westin/grandbohemian

Price Range: $$$

The Orlando Grand Bohemian is blocks from the Orlando Expo Center, and a 20-minute drive from Disneyland. Those seeking a diversion from the Magic Kingdom can leash-up their dogs and head to Lake Eola Park, a popular attraction four blocks from the hotel. Circle the lake and you've walked just under a mile. Dogs must be on-leash at all times, and kept from mingling with the swans. Back at the hotel, you can enjoy rare artwork at the gallery as well as steak and seafood at the Boheme. As your pup snoozes on her dog bed, cap off the night with a decaf something-or-other from the in-house Starbucks. $100 fee. 20-pound weight limit.

(561) – Palm Beach & Manalapan

Brazilian Court

(561) 655-7740
301 Australian Ave (between Cocoanut Row & Hibiscus Ave)
Palm Beach, Florida 33480
www.thebraziliancourt.com

Price Range: $$$$

Palm Beach is where the rich go to play, and many stay at the Spanish-style Brazilian Court. While this exquisite Palm Beach hideaway is a Leading Small Hotels of the World member, it does have just one problem: renovations. Its elegant courtyards and reputation must be maintained, and the process may interfere with your stay. Your dog is still welcome and should sleep fine on the hotel-provided dog bed. $100 fee. No weight limit.

Chesterfield Hotel

(561) 659 5800
363 Coconut Row (@ Royal Palm Bridge)
Palm Beach, Florida 33480
www.slh.com/chesterfield

Price Range: $$$$

This landmark hotel, built in 1926, was remodeled four years ago to create an exotic Mediterranean exterior and sophisticated British interior. The library, tranquil courtyard and elegant, antique-filled lobby are luxurious without being stuffy. The hotel will provide your pet with food, water, a bed and toy. The hotel also offers referrals to local shops for dog walking services, day care and grooming. The beach is just three blocks away and allows leashed dogs. $100 deposit, and a $50 fee. 40-pound weight limit.

Four Seasons Resort: Palm Beach

(561) 582-2800
2800 S Ocean Blvd (north of Lake Worth Rd)
Palm Beach, Florida 33480
www.fourseasons.com/palmbeach

Price Range: $$$$$

Just a stone's throw from the ocean, this resort epitomizes luxury. The on-site spa features a host of skin-care treatments, body wraps and massage. Guests can play a game of golf or tennis, or just sit poolside. And kids' services include arts and crafts, video games and sea turtle watching. Dogs are treated to bones and bowls, walks on a nearby jogging trail and a room service menu for pets that includes hamburgers and rice, or chicken and pasta. Pets aren't allowed in the rooms unattended, so take your pup with you or prepare to pay a pet-sitter $16 per hour with a four-hour minimum. No fee. 15-pound weight limit.

(727) - Palm Harbor

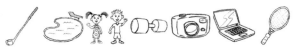

The Westin: Innisbrook Golf Resort

(727) 942-2000
36750 N US Hwy 19
(@ Alderman Rd)
Palm Harbor, Florida 34684
www.starwood.com/westin/innisbrook

Price Range: $$$$$

Dogs are welcome almost anywhere on the dazzling grounds
of this all-suite Westin resort; just keep them off the hotel's 72
holes of championship golf and the practice fields. For less
manicured surroundings, take your pet to Honeymoon Island
State Park. Park rangers ask only that you keep your pet leashed
and pick up after him. While you're out enjoying the hotel's
waterslide complex, be aware that housekeeping won't come
in if your dog is in the room alone. This family-friendly hotel
also offers numerous pools, one called the Loch Ness, as well
as a giant, poolside sandbox. $50 fee. 50-pound weight limit.

(941) - Sarasota

The Ritz Carlton: Sarasota

(941) 309-2000
1111 Ritz-Carlton Dr
(between US 41 & Gulfstream Ave)
Sarasota, Florida 34236
www.ritzcarlton.com/resorts/sarasota

Price Range: $$$$$

This Ritz is all about the beach. The hotel restaurant serves
fresh seafood from the Gulf, and suites feature views of
Sarasota Bay. Offerings include beach activities just for kids,
and spa services so unique, spa aficionados may feel like a

neophyte. There's also sunning on the private beach—an area that is unfortunately off-limits to dogs. But your pet is welcome on the 40 miles of hiking trails at Myakka River State Park. The hotel staff will walk your dog around the block. Dogs are permitted to stay alone in the room but must be crated for housekeeping. For a fee, this Ritz provides dog dishes and bones. $125 fee. 30-pound weight limit.

Georgia

(404) - Atlanta

Four Seasons Hotel: Atlanta
The Ritz-Carlton: Buckhead
The Westin: Atlanta Airport
The Westin: Buckhead Atlanta
The Westin: Peachtree Plaza

(770) - Atlanta & Adairsville

Barnsley Gardens Resort
W: Atlanta
The Westin: Atlanta North at Perimeter

(912) - Savannah

The Westin: Savannah Harbor Golf Resort & Spa

(404) - Atlanta

Four Seasons Hotel: Atlanta
(404) 881-9898
75 14th St
(between W Peachtree St & Crescent Ave)
Atlanta, Georgia 30309
www.fourseasons.com/atlanta
Price Range: $$$$$
Chandeliers, vaulted ceilings and in-laid marble flooring give
this Four Seasons the feel of a grand ballroom. The rooms are
tastefully decorated in subdued colors and the skyscraper
design makes for breathtaking views of downtown Atlanta.
Perks include a state-of-the-art fitness center, lap pool, sauna,
steam room, massages and body treatments. Several golf
courses and a tennis club are close by. The hotel restaurant,
Park 75—known for its Sunday brunch—offers an eight-course
meal at the Chef's table. Your pup receives freshly baked dog
biscuits, bowls, walks in nearby Piedmont Park ($15 per 30

minute walk) and a room-service menu featuring chopped steak. No fee. 25-pound weight limit.

The Ritz-Carlton: Buckhead

(404) 237-2700
3434 Peachtree Rd NE (@ Lenox Rd NE)
Atlanta, Georgia 30326
www.ritzcarlton.com/hotels/atlanta_buckhead
Price Range: $$$$$

Long regarded as a landmark in uptown Atlanta, the Ritz-Carlton Buckhead is surrounded by the area's financial district, sophisticated dining and entertainment—plus two of the Southeast's most prestigious malls: Phipps Plaza and Lenox Square. The concierge will coordinate dog care and walks. Book your dog a half-hour jaunt with a treat afterwards, while you treat yourself to the Ritz's exotic tea service—red, white, green and black teas from China, Ceylon, Egypt and Spain (lavender, cinnamon or tangerine scents optional). $250 fee. 30-pound weight limit.

The Westin: Atlanta Airport

(404) 762-7676
4736 Best Rd (@ T Owen Smith Blvd)
Atlanta, Georgia 30337
www.starwood.com/westin/atlantaairport
Price Range: $$$

This Westin is very dog-friendly as long as you alert them in advance. Upon arrival, prepare to be amazed at the 10-story lobby atrium—a magnificent mass of marble, glass and green-ery. The front desk will have a dog bed and bowls waiting for you, and rooms also come with a fax, printer, copier and high-speed Internet access. There are two restaurants on-site, plus 24-hour room service and a Starbucks kiosk that serves Krispy Kreme doughnuts and Little Caesar's pizza. There are no parks nearby, but there are some grassy areas on the grounds. No fee. No weight limit.

The Westin: Buckhead Atlanta

(404) 365-0065
3391 NE Peachtree Rd
(@ Lenox Rd)
Atlanta, Georgia 30326
www.starwood.com/westin/buckhead
Price Range: **$$$**
You're in the middle of splendor at this 22-story, dog-friendly
Atlanta landmark. Your room includes a large desk, Starbucks
coffee as well as floor-to-ceiling windows that show off the
Buckhead skyline. You're also steps from the Southeast's most
revered shopping malls: the Lenox Mall and Phipps Plaza, also
two of the best places for dog-walks. The hotel grounds offer
grassy patches fit for your dog, and if you give advance notice,
the hotel staff will have a Westin Heavenly Dog Bed ready for
your pup. $250 deposit. 40-pound weight limit.

The Westin: Peachtree Plaza

(404) 659-1400
210 Peachtree St
(@ Andrew Young Int'l)
Atlanta, Georgia 30303
www.starwood.com/westin/peachtree
Price Range: **$$$**
With 73 floors overlooking Atlanta's business and financial dis-
trict, a glass elevator going up to the Sun Dial and a revolving
restaurant offering 360-degree city views, Westin's Peachtree
Plaza is quite a sight. The hotel welcomes your pet with a bed
and directions to the Centennial Olympic Park, just a few minutes away. Just be sure to register your dog beforehand. And if
you're out sightseeing at the nearby CNN Center or Coca-Cola
Museum, both six blocks away, your dog can be left in the
room alone. Just let the front desk know so they can alert the
housekeeping staff. No fee. 40-pound weight limit.

(770) - Atlanta & Adairsville

Barnsley Gardens Resort

(770) 773-7480
597 Barnsley Gardens Rd
(@ Hall Station Rd)
Adairsville, Georgia 30103
www.slh.com/usa/adairsville/hotel_adabar.html

Price Range: $$$$$

Prepare to be transported back in time when you enter this 19th century English village with old-world streets and country cottages, tucked in the foothills of the Blue Ridge Mountains. Modern amenities include a championship golf course and full-service spa, plus clay tennis courts, fishing ponds, gardens and trails for hiking and horseback riding. In-house dining includes the Rice House Restaurant featuring traditional Southern cooking, the Woodlands Grill steakhouse and the Bavarian Beer Garden with an open fire pit. A $75 flat fee includes a dog bed, food and a toy. There's a two-dog max, but the second one stays free. No weight limit.

W: Atlanta

(770) 396-6800
111 W Perimeter Center
(near NE Perimeter Center Pkwy)
Atlanta, Georgia 30346
www.starwood.com/whotels/atlanta

Price Range: $$$$$

Located in an upscale suburb near the Buckhead business district, the W Atlanta at Perimeter Center is known for the daily lobby promenades of guests showing off their pets. Your pup is welcome on the hotel's one-acre green knoll, or you can head to Piedmont Park—a posh off-leash dog park in downtown Atlanta. Amenities include a welcome package including a toy, gourmet treats, W Hotel pet tag, clean up bags and in-room dog necessities: pet bed, food and water bowls, Pet in

Room sign and a turn-down treat as well as essential dog-care referrals. $100 cleaning fee, plus a $25 per night charge. 60-pound weight limit.

The Westin: Atlanta North at Perimeter
(770) 395-3900
7 Concourse Pkwy NE
(off Hammond Dr)
Atlanta, Georgia 30328
www.starwood.com/westin/atlantanorth
Price Range: $$$
This contemporary Westin offers a haven of tranquility in close proximity to downtown. Located on a private lake—a great place to walk your dog—the hotel is adjacent to the country's fourth largest health facility. The Concourse Athletic Club offers indoor running, racquetball along with weights and cardio. As a Westin guest, you exercise for free. You can take in the water view at the hotel's Lakeside Grill and the 60 acres of unspoiled woodland—another great place to take your pup. Just be sure to take a pooper scooper to keep it pristine. The Westin provides pups with bowls and its Heavenly Dog Bed. $25 fee, plus a $75 refundable deposit. 20-pound weight limit.

(912) - Savannah

The Westin: Savannah Harbor Golf Resort & Spa
(912) 201-2000
1 Resort Dr
(@ Wayne Shackleford Blvd)
Savannah, Georgia 31421
www.starwood.com/westin/savannah
Price Range: $$$

A mix of old-world charm and modern technology, this Westin resort on the exclusive Hutchinson Island, is a dog-friendly palace. The dog floor on level five also offers magnificent views of the Savannah River and the city's historic district. Your pup gets bowls and a bed, plus a pooper scooper—a welcome accessory as you and your pet explore the resort's magnificent grounds. People perks include an 18-hole championship golf course designed by Sam Snead, a full-service spa, a riverside hot tub and charter fishing. $50 fee. 40-pound weight limit.

Illinois

(312) - Chicago

Four Seasons Hotel: Chicago
Hotel 71
Hotel Allegro
Hotel Monaco: Chicago
The Ritz-Carlton: Chicago
Sofitel: Chicago Water Tower
Sutton Place Hotel
Talbott Hotel
The Westin: Chicago River North
The Westin: Michigan Avenue Chicago
The Whitehall Hotel

(847) - Rosemont

Sofitel: Chicago O'Hare
The Westin: O'Hare

(312) - Chicago

Four Seasons Hotel: Chicago
(312) 280-8800
120 E Delaware Pl
(between Emst Ct & N Lake Shore Dr)
Chicago, Illinois 60611
www.fourseasons.com/chicagofs
Price Range: $$$$$
The Chicago Four Seasons—part swanky bar and part grand
ballroom—combines elegance with a bit of jazz: one particu-
lar highlight is the huge Roman pool under a glass dome.
Other perks include a fitness center, a sauna, steam room and
an array of spa services: Try the Crushed Pearls and Lavender
Body Polish. The hotel's Seasons, named Chicago's most
romantic restaurant, serves French-American cuisine. Just steps

from the posh shops on Michigan Avenue and close to golf and tennis facilities, this Four Seasons offers something for everyone, even your pup. Dog perks include a room-service menu, featuring breakfast bacon treats. No fee. 15-pound weight limit.

Hotel 71
(800) 621-4005
71 E Wacker Dr
(@ Michigan Ave)
Chicago, Illinois 60601
www.hotel71.com
Price Range: $$$$

This hotel, which is swarming with hipsters and fashionistas, is so swanky, you'd think they only accept designer dogs. However, they accommodate all dogs under 45 pounds. There's no fee to have your pup stay with you, but you're on your own when it comes to dog supplies and amenities. The hotel is just off Magnificent Mile, a great place to go for a window-shopping walk. Critics warn: If your idea of serenity is silence, this might not be the best place for you.

Hotel Allegro
(866) 672-6143
171 W Randolph St
(@ La Salle St)
Chicago, Illinois 60601
www.allegrochicago.com
Price Range: $$$

Color takes on new meaning at Hotel Allegro, where bright colors bring plush, comfy accommodations to life. Like all Kimpton hotels, the Allegro is known for outstanding service as well as its evening wine hour. The Allegro also boasts Italian fare at 312 Chicago; cocktails and lunch at Encore; and the off-site Spa Space, which made Oprah's O-List. Pet offerings include the optional Happy Tails VIP package with treats, a toy and a guidebook to teach the techniques of dog massage. You may also request a bed, food bowls, a Frisbee or even a raincoat for your dog. The bellman will walk your pup and the concierge can arrange pet-sitting. No fee. No weight limit.

Hotel Monaco: Chicago
(866) 610-0081
225 N Wabash Ave
(@ Wacker Dr)
Chicago, Illinois 60601
www.monaco-chicago.com
Price Range: $$$
The French-deco design of this boutique hotel is fanciful, festive and inviting. The evening wine hour, standard at all Kimpton hotels, will make the most tentative traveler feel welcome. Room offerings include more than the usual bath products, exquisite linens, as well as 24/7 in-room televised yoga instruction. Purchase the PAWS Chicago package and 10 percent of the proceeds will be donated to PAWS. The package includes a welcome letter from Oscar, the hotel's resident dog, a dog bed, bowl and bone at turn-down. The concierge will arrange for dog walking, pet-sitting, grooming or spa services. Make sure to sign the pet register before you leave. No fee. No weight limit.

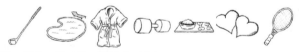

The Ritz-Carlton: Chicago
(312) 266-1000
160 E Pearson St
(off N Michigan Ave)
Chicago, Illinois 60611
www.fourseasons.com/chicagorc
Price Range: $$$$$
Owned by the Four Seasons, this Ritz could have been lifted from a 1930s French boudoir—complete with satin chairs, frilly lampshades and floral tapestries. Perks include a lap

pool, fitness center with trainers and a sundeck. Golf and tennis are also nearby. Massages, body treatments, facials and manicures are available through the spa. Make your reservations in advance for the award-winning Dining Room, it received four stars from both the *Chicago Tribune* and *Chicago* magazine. Your pup will receive a bed, bowls and snacks: Just be sure to call ahead. No fee. 30-pound weight limit.

Sofitel: Chicago Water Tower
(312) 324-4000
20 E Chestnut St
(@ Michigan Ave)
Chicago, Illinois 60611
www.sofitel.com
Price Range: $$$
Your pup will receive a treat upon arrival at this new Sofitel. While minimalist in decor, this hotel exudes a warmth usually only felt in boutique hotels. Sofitel's Le Bar is downright funky, while Cafe Des Architects (a nod to Sofitel architect Jean Paul Viguier) is more elegant. And the wood-tiled walls are the perfect backdrop for the serene bedrooms. Grant Park, Millennium Park and the scenic Lake Michigan waterfront are just a stone's throw away. If the exploring wears your pup out out, the nearby Streeterville Pet Spa & Boutique will rejuvenate her. No fee. 20-pound weight limit.

Sutton Place Hotel
(800) 606-8188
21 E Bellevue Pl
(@ N State St)
Chicago, Illinois 60611
www.suttonplace.com/spghg_chi.htm
Price Range: $$$$
This contemporary hotel underwent a renovation in 2003 to modernize its AAA four-diamond rooms. In the process, the guestrooms were made more comfortable. Your pet can sneak

a treat from the doorman on his way out, and the hotel concierge will schedule any pet-sitting or dog walking services during your stay. $200 deposit. 20-pound weight limit.

Talbott Hotel
(800) 825-2688
20 E Delaware Pl
(between State St & Wabash Ave)
Chicago, Illinois 60611
www.talbotthotel.com
Price Range: $$$$

Enjoy Rush Street nightlife, Michigan Avenue shopping and walks along the lake—all just steps from the boutique Talbott Hotel. The hotel, which began allowing pets in 2004, offers an in-room pet menu full of treats. Just make sure to bring your own supplies and arrange for someone to walk your dog while you're out. The hotel does not offer dog walking or sitting. $25 fee. 25-pound weight limit.

The Westin: Chicago River North
(312) 744-1900
320 N Dearborn St
(@ Clark St)
Chicago, Illinois 60610
www.starwood.com/westin/rivernorth
Price Range: $$$

The Westin Chicago River North, located in the heart of the city's business and theatre district, offers eclectic food at Ember Grille as well as cocktails and imported cigars at the Hana Lounge. Several dog-friendly spots are nearby, including Millennium Park, which features landscape design and interactive public art. Dogs are even allowed off leash on parts of Lake Front Trail at the beach. If you want to do a little shopping, Michigan Avenue and Magnificent Mile—two of Chicago's best shopping strips—are both four blocks away. Most importantly: Wiggly Field Dog Park is a short cab ride away and well worth the trip. No fee. 25-pound weight limit.

The Westin: Michigan Avenue Chicago

(312) 943-7200
909 N Michigan Ave
(@ Delaware Pl)
Chicago, Illinois 60611
www.starwood.com/michiganave

Price Range: $$$

On Chicago's Magnificent Mile, the Westin sits across the street from the shops at the Water Tower Plaza and Bloomingdale's. Many other sites are also within walking distance, and some are dog-friendly—including Grant and Millennium parks. Three blocks from the hotel at Lake Michigan, your dog has beach privileges. If you need a treat, check out the Westin's Salon-Pusha D'Europe, which offers skin treatments, manicures, hair styling and make-up application. Westin dog amenities include the signature Westin Heavenly Dog Bed and bowls. $25 per day. Two dog max per room. No weight limit.

The Whitehall Hotel

(312) 944 6300
105 E Delaware Pl
(@ Rush St)
Chicago, Illinois 60611
www.slh.com/whitehall

Price Range: $$$$

Declared "one of eight great small hotels in the U.S." by *Fortune* magazine, this boutique hotel offers traditional European-style rooms that are richly appointed with plush, floral bedding and valances. Those wishing to take advantage of Magnificent Mile's shopping, dining and museums will appreciate the Whitehall's Gold Coast location. The lakefront is just beyond the shops on Michigan Avenue, so leash-up your dog and head over for a stroll along the water. Remember: Dogs aren't allowed in the lake. $100 partially refundable deposit. 30-pound weight limit.

(847) - Rosemont

Sofitel: Chicago O'Hare

(847) 678-4488
5550 N River Rd (@ Bryn Mawr Ave)
Rosemont, Illinois 60018
www.sofitel.com
Price Range: $$$

If you want to stay near the airport, this is one of the few
hotels that allows dogs. The classically comfy rooms are a
great place to relax, and the staff happily caters to any whim
you might have. If you're in town for a trade show there is a
skyway connecting the hotel to the Rosemont Convention
Center—helpful if it's raining or you have a lot to carry. There's
not much nearby in the way of off-leash space so your pup
may have to go without the daily run. Be careful when you do
take your dog outdoors, the hotel's parking lot stays busy. $25
fee, plus $50 deposit. No weight limit.

The Westin: O'Hare

(847) 698-6000
6100 River Rd (@ Higgins Rd)
Rosemont, Illinois 60618
www.westinohare.com
Price Range: $$$

Only five minutes from O'Hare International Airport, this
Westin offers all kinds of exercise for you and your pet. Your
workout options at the hotel's enormous fitness center include
weights, racquetball, basketball, an indoor swimming pool
and cardiovascular machines—each equipped with a TV.
Leashed dogs are welcome to walk through the lobby and
other hotel areas. Your pup has access to plenty of grass and
there's a walking trail in the forest preserve located behind the
hotel. Hotel dining options include the Benchmark Bistro and
the Bakery/Coffee Counter. The hotel provides your pup with
a signature Westin Heavenly Dog Bed. No fee. 40-pound
weight limit.

Indiana

(317) – Indianapolis

The Westin: Indianapolis

The Westin: Indianapolis
(317) 262-8100
50 S Capitol Ave
(between Washington & Maryland sts)
Indianapolis, Indiana 46204
www.starwood.com/westin/indianapolis
Price Range: $$$
This downtown Indianapolis Westin is attached via skybridge
to hundreds of shops at Circle Center Mall. And the RCA
Dome, home of the Indianapolis Colts, is only a block away.
Dog amenities include the Westin's signature Heavenly Dog
Bed. If your dog needs exercise, stroll through White River
State Park, a local hidden treasure with a half-mile path along
the water. On your walk you'll see the landmark Rose
Window, a hand-carved limestone structure. No fee. 40-
pound weight limit.

Louisiana

(504) - New Orleans

Hotel Monaco: New Orleans
The Iberville Suites
The Ritz-Carlton:New Orleans
W: New Orleans – French Quarter
W: New Orleans- Riverwalk
Windsor Court Hotel

(504) - New Orleans

Hotel Monaco: New Orleans
(866) 685-8359
333 St. Charles Ave (between Union & Perdido sts)
New Orleans, Louisiana 70130
www.monaco-neworleans.com
Price Range: $$$
The exquisite Hotel Monaco New Orleans stays true to the history of its domicile, which was constructed in 1926 as a Masonic temple. Its architecture is full of earthier tones, unlike other Monaco outposts which lean toward a fun, funky and vibrant color palate. People perks include evening wine hour, a standard at Kimpton Hotels. The optional Bone Appetite package includes a dog toy, tags, bed, treats and water bowl filled with Evian, a map to the nearest dog-friendly park and a $5 coupon to the Three Dog Bakery. One free walk is included in the package, or you can always ask the concierge to arrange for a pet-sitter. No fee. No weight limit.

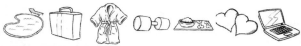

The Iberville Suites

(866) 229-4351
904 Rue Iberville (between Dauphine & Burgundy sts)
New Orleans, Louisiana 70112
www.ibervillesuites.com

Price Range: $$$

On the edge of the French Quarter, this gracious boutique hotel is managed by, and shares a building with, the Ritz Carlton. And Iberville guests have spa and charging privileges at the Ritz. Even without the R-C perks, the Iberville's suite-style rooms, gorgeous hardwood floors, floor-to-ceiling windows and exquisite antique collection, make it quite pleasing. This hotel also provides a nice retreat after a long day—and night—of excitement in the French Quarter. The neighborhood offers scenic dog walks. Be sure to try the dog take-out at the Ritz-recommended Three Dog Bakery. $125 fee. 40-pound weight limit.

The Ritz-Carlton: New Orleans

(504) 524-1331
921 Canal St
(between Dauphine & Burgundy sts)
New Orleans, Louisiana 70112
www.ritzcarlton.com/hotels/new_orleans

Price Range: $$$$$

With the graciousness and mystery of a classic antebellum mansion, this Ritz boasts easy living in the Big Easy. If you give the hotel advance notice of your dog's arrival, the staff will be ready with a dog bed, bowl, chew toys and a leash. The concierge will coordinate dog-walking and pet-sitting services through Helen's Happy Housepets. You and your pet can also stroll through the French Quarter to Waldenberg Park, a local landmark six blocks away that overlooks the Mississippi River. Hotel offerings include an award-winning spa, a ballroom and boardrooms, along with several golf courses within a half-hour's drive. $125 fee. 40-pound weight limit.

W: New Orleans – French Quarter
(504) 581-1200
316 Chartres St
(@ Bienville Ave)
New Orleans, Louisiana 70130
www.starwood.com/whotels/frenchquarter
Price Range: $$$$

The French Quarter W is best described as plantation chic with a minimalist W twist. The decor includes plush velvet crimson drapes that double as living room/lobby walls. The hotel is close to Waldenberg Park, the Three Dog Bakery and the historic Garden District—perfect for a walk with your pup. Your dog's welcome gift includes a toy, gourmet treat, W Hotel pet tag and baggies. In-room dog necessities include a pet bed, Woof food and water bowls, Pet in Room sign and turn-down treat, plus a list of essential service referrals. Room service will supply forgotten leashes, toys, food or treats. $25 nightly fee, plus a $100 cleaning fee. No weight limit.

W: New Orleans – Riverwalk
(504) 525-9444
333 Poydras St
(@ S Peters St)
New Orleans, Louisiana 70130
www.starwood.com/whotels/neworleans
Price Range: $$$$

This tall, modern W sits on the buoyant Riverwalk, a half-mile marketplace alongside the Mississippi River. As sleek on the inside as it is on the outside, the hotel is home to Zoe Restaurant, W Cafe and Rande Gerber's bar, Whiskey Blue, which is a local hot spot. Amenities include a welcome package (toy, gourmet treat, W Hotel pet tag, cleanup bags), in-room dog necessities (pet bed, Woof food and water bowls, Pet in Room sign, turn-down treat) and essential service referrals. Room service will bring you anything from leashes and toys to food and treats. $125 fee. 80-pound weight limit.

Windsor Court Hotel

(888) 596-0955
300 Gravier St
(@ S Peters St)
New Orleans, Louisiana 70130
www.windsorcourthotel.com

Price Range: $$$

This elegant Orient Express hotel is a regular fixture on the
Condé Nast Gold List and *Travel & Leisure's* 100 Best Hotels as
well as one of *Departures* magazine's 25 Best Business Hotels.
With an English country-house feel, the Windsor comes com-
plete with a lavish courtyard, high tea and an art gallery. The
first hotel in the area to accept pets, the Windsor is quite dog
friendly. In addition to offering a Windsor Court bowl and gour-
met treats, the hotel staff will walk your dog for you. The
concierge can also direct you to a great off-leash park a short
drive away. $150 fee. 50-pound weight limit.

Maine

(207) – Cape Elizabeth

Inn by the Sea

Inn by the Sea
(800) 888-4287
40 Bowery Beach Rd
(@ Route 77)
Cape Elizabeth, Maine   04107
www.innbythesea.com
Price Range: $$$$$
Boasting oceanfront suites and cottages, Inn by the Sea offers
laidback luxury for the whole family, including your dog. In
addition to the beach, pool and tennis courts, guests have
access to a private golf course and local gym. Dog offerings
include bowls and a bed, as well as a dog menu with such
dishes as Satin Balls (for dogs on raw diets), chicken, a sirloin
burger and homemade biscuits. Crescent Beach State Park
allows dogs only in the off-season. However, there are several
off-leash dog parks a short drive away. The Inn needs advance
notice of dog guests as well as services your pet might need.
No fee. No weight limit.

Maryland

(410) - St. Michaels

The Inn at Perry Cabin

The Inn at Perry Cabin
(800) 722-2949
308 Watkins Ln
(@ Talbot St)
St. Michaels, Maryland 21663
www.perrycabin.com
Price Range: $$$$$
A regular on the *Condé Nast Traveler* Gold List, this Orient
Express romantic manor-house resort is considered the finest
hotel on the Eastern Shore. Activities include sailing, bicycling,
swimming in their heated horizon-edge pool and golf. Pet
amenities include a canine menu, which features osso bucco
with seasonal vegetables and freshly prepared treats as well as
canine turn-down service. Dog-walking and sitting services are
also available. In the surrounding area, you'll find state parks,
beaches and off-leash green spaces—including Assateague
Park, which hosts herds of wild ponies. Flying Fred's Pet
Boutique is next door, and the hotel hosts annual Jack Russell
terrier races. $75 fee per pet. 75-pound weight limit.

Massachusetts

(617) - Boston, Cambridge

Charles Hotel
The Eliot Hotel
Fifteen Beacon
Four Seasons Hotel: Boston
Hotel Commonwealth
Hotel Marlowe
Langham Hotel
Nine Zero Hotel
Onyx Hotel
The Ritz-Carlton: Boston
The Ritz-Carlton: Boston Common
Seaport Hotel
The Westin: Copley Place

(978) - Salem

The Hawthorne Hotel

(781) - Waltham

The Westin: Waltham-Boston

(617) - Boston, Cambridge

Charles Hotel
(617) 864-1200
1 Bennett St
(@ Brattle St)
Cambridge, Massachusetts 02138
www.charleshotel.com
Price Range: $$$$
Guest packages abound this unique luxury hotel that overlooks Harvard Square: One even includes a free tank of gas
before departure. Other perks include a health club, indoor

pool and day spa, as well as award-winning in-house restaurants and entertainment: Henrietta's Table was *Boston* magazine's 2000 pick for Best Breakfast. Rialto made *Food and Wine* magazine's Top 50 Hotel Restaurants in America list. The hotel is also home to the Regattabar Jazz Club as well as the lobby bar, Noir. If you feel like a trip to adjacent Boston, the hotel will make dog-sitting arrangements (with eight-hours notice). $50 fee. No weight limit.

The Eliot Hotel
(800) 443-5468
370 Commonwealth Ave
(@ Massachusetts Ave)
Boston, Massachusetts 02215
www.eliothotel.com
Price Range: $$$$
The elegant Eliot Hotel is conveniently located in the Back Bay within walking distance of Fenway Park, Newberry Street, Symphony Hall, Copley Square and the Public Gardens. Boston medical centers, MIT, the financial and theater districts and Logan airport are also nearby. You will not be without places to walk your dog: A good thing too, since dogs aren't allowed alone in the room. However, the hotel provides pet-sitting services. The Eliot is home to the renowned restaurant Clio, which offers Asian-inspired French cuisine as well as Uni sashimi bar. Perks include privileges at the Boston Sports Club. No fee. No weight limit.

Fifteen Beacon
(877) 982-3226
15 Beacon St
(between Bowdoin & Somerset sts)
Boston, Massachusetts 02108
www.XVbeacon.com
Price Range: $$$$
From *Condé Nast Traveler*, *Travel & Leisure*, *Departures* and

the *Robb Report*, to *Boston* magazine and *Wine Spectator*, to City Search and Expedia, XV Beacon is on all of the best- and top-hotel lists. It has received endless accolades for everything from its wine list to its wait staff and lobster bisque. No two of the elegantly appointed guestrooms are alike. The sleek white-and-black decor is crisp and comfortable. Well-behaved dogs under 20 pounds are welcome at no additional charge. However, you will be responsible for any damage done to the pristine white linens, carpet and furnishings. Pets can't be left unattended unless crated.

Four Seasons Hotel: Boston

(617) 338-4400
200 Boylston St
(@ Park Pl)
Boston, Massachusetts 02216
www.fourseasons7.com/boston

Price Range: $$$$$

Teeming with old world charm, the Four Seasons Hotel—a regular on the *Condé Nast Traveler* Gold List—is one of the best hotels in Boston. Your pup will also experience the exceptional service and accommodations the Four Seasons is so famous for. He'll receive freshly baked dog biscuits upon arrival as well as a bowl and sleeping pad. There's even a room-service menu for dogs, featuring items like the Rin-Tin-Tin (scrambled hamburger and egg). One thing to keep in mind: This Four Seasons does not allow pets to stay in the room unattended, so prepare to pay $16 an hour for a pet-sitter. Otherwise, dogs stay for free. 15-pound weight limit.

Hotel Commonwealth
(866) 784-4000
500 Commonwealth Ave (@ Beacon St)
Boston, Massachusetts 02215
www.slh.com/commonwealth
Price Range: $$$

Modern technology—including wireless Internet throughout the hotel—is the only thing that belies the timeless ambience of this Kenmore Square hotel, which was recently built in 2002. The oversized rooms are exquisitely appointed, offering all the creature comforts one should be so lucky as to have in their home. Dog amenities and services include nightly turn-down service with bedtime treats as well as bowls for food and water. The concierge will coordinate dog-walking and day-care services through affiliated businesses in the area. The hotel is within walking distance of the fabled Fenway Park and Boston University, as well as Boston's hospitals. $25 fee. 25-pound weight limit.

Hotel Marlowe
(800) 825-7140
25 Edwin H. Land Blvd (@ Charles St)
Cambridge, Massachusetts 02141
www.hotelmarlowe.com
Price Range: $$$$$

The design—high-end funky—blends seamlessly with the architecture of this historic hotel just off Newbury Street. At $75, the Man's Best Friend Pampering Kit—which includes a dog bed, fleece blanket and lunch box with gourmet dog cookies—is hard to pass up. Treat your dog to a night at the Hotel Marlowe on his birthday, and the hotel will order him a cake from Polka Dog Bakery. People perks include a business center, free wireless Internet throughout the hotel and 24-hour room service courtesy of the hotel-adjacent Bambara restaurant. Minglers will enjoy the evening wine hour in the hotel lobby (a standard at Kimpton hotels). No fee. 30-pound weight limit.

Langham Hotel

(617) 451-1900
250 Franklin St (between Oliver & Pearl sts)
Boston, Massachusetts 02110
www.langhamhotels.com/langham/boston
Price Range: $$$$

A member of the Leading Hotels of the World, the grand
Langham Hotel Boston—whose domicile was formerly a
Federal Reserve Bank—is listed on the National Registry of
Historic Places. It overlooks Boston Harbor, Faneuil Hall and
the spectacular park at Post Office Square where you can take
your dog (on-leash) and laptop. Wireless Internet access is
available throughout the park. Well-behaved dogs may be left
unattended, or pet sitting can be arranged. Leashes are required
throughout the property. $50 fee. 50-pound weight limit.

The Nine Zero Hotel

(617) 772-5800
90 Tremont St (between Beacon & Park sts)
Boston, Massachusetts 02108
www.ninezero.com
Price Range: $$$$$

Landing *Boston* magazine's coveted Best Boutique Hotel title
for 2003 as well as a nice spot on the *Condé Nast Traveler*
Gold List, Nine Zero offers travelers the perfect combination of
business conveniences and pampering amenities—including
an in-room yoga channel as well as Pilates instruction, buck-
wheat pillows and free high-speed Internet access. The hotel is
on Freedom Trail and within walking distance of Faneuil Hall,
Boston Gardens and Newbury Street. Dogs are gifted on
arrival with the In the Dog House package of treats and bowls.
In-room amenities include a dog bed and room-service menu
just for pups. The concierge will arrange for dog-sitting and
walking, grooming and massage. No fee. No weight limit.

Onyx Hotel

(617) 557-9955
155 Portland St (off Causeway St)
Boston, Massachusetts 02114
www.onyxhotel.com
Price Range: $$$

The sleek white-and-black decor of the uber-hip Onyx Hotel is brought to life by perfectly placed ruby-red accents. This Kimpton hotel is near Fleet Center, Faneuil Hall, City Hall and Bunker Hill. Dog offerings include gourmet dog treats and the hotel will arrange for dog walking and pet-sitting. People should enjoy the the evening wine hour in the lobby. Fun fact: the Onyx was the official hotel of Britney Spears' short-lived 2004 Onyx Hotel Tour. Die-hard Britney fans can book the Britney Spears Foundation Room, which features sparkling wallpaper. Everyone else will be satisfied with the plush decor of their usual rooms. No fee. No weight limit.

The Ritz-Carlton: Boston

(617) 536-5700
15 Arlington St (@ Newbury St)
Boston, Massachusetts 02116
www.ritzcarlton.com/hotels/boston
Price Range: $$$$$

Offering guests a world of crystal chandeliers and wood-burning fireplaces (complete with a butler to light the fire)—the Boston Ritz, a *Condé Nast Traveler* Gold List pick, integrates yesteryear elegance with 21st-century service. Dog amenities include a dish, water bowl, treats and a bed. They offer pet meals too, delivered daily and prepared by the chef: The Lassie meal, a shepherd's pie for dogs, is a favorite. When you're out—possibly across the street at Boston Public Garden or nearby at Boston Common—you can't leave your dog alone in the room. The concierge will arrange for pet-sitting. $35 nightly fee per pet. 20-pound weight limit.

The Ritz-Carlton: Boston Common

(617) 574-7100
10 Avery St
(@ Tremont St)
Boston, Massachusetts 02111
www.ritzcarlton.com/hotels/boston_common

Price Range: $$$$$

A reserve on the *Condé Nast Traveler* Gold List, this Ritz at
Boston Common sits directly across from Boston's other Ritz.
Contemporary and cosmopolitan, with a restaurant featuring
classic American cuisine, the hotel offers upscale amenities for
pets too. Get the deluxe or executive suite and your dog gets
the Pampered Pet Package: biscuits, cobalt-blue water bowl
and a one-hour beauty treatment—including grooming and
massage. You can combine sightseeing with dog walking by
taking a hike on the nearby Freedom Trail, which offers two-
plus miles of historic sites with a red line along the sidewalk
that points the way. $50 per-pet fee. No weight limit.

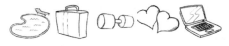

Seaport Hotel

(877) 732-7678
1 Seaport Ln
(@ Northern Ave)
Boston, Massachusetts 02210
www.seaportboston.com

Price Range: $$$

Touting itself as the most accommodating host in Boston, the
Seaport is non-smoking, gratuity-free and happy to help with
anything you and your pet need during your stay. Although the
Seaport doesn't provide any standard pet-amenity packages,
they do honor special requests—free of charge. The waterfront
location offers pleasant walks, or you can head to the on-leash
Marine Industrial Park. For off-leash fun, Columbia Park is a
10-minute drive away. Dogs aren't allowed alone in the room,
but the hotel staff will make pet-sitting arrangements. No fee.
50-pound weight limit.

The Westin: Copley Place

(617) 262-9600
10 Huntington Ave
(@ Dartmouth St)
Boston, Massachusetts 02116
www.starwood.com/westin/copleyplace

Price Range: $$$

Located in the historic Back Bay, one of the best neighborhoods in Boston, the Westin is only a skywalk away from 100 of the most sophisticated shops and boutiques in the Northeast and across the street from Copley Square—a local dog hot spot. It sports big grassy areas and plenty of room for your leashed dog to roam. Pet amenities are limited to the Westin's signature Heavenly Dog Bed. The hotel boasts three top restaurants along with Bar 10. $100 deposit. 40-pound weight limit.

(978) - Salem

The Hawthorne Hotel

(800) 729-7829
18 W Washington Sq
(@ Essex St)
Salem, Massachusetts 01970
www.hawthornehotel.com

Price Range: $$$

This stately hotel in the Salem Common Historic District is surrounded by must-see landmarks—including the Salem Witch Museum. Dogs receive a welcome pack upon arrival with bowls, treats and a pet room-service menu. October is one of the best months to visit the reportedly haunted Hawthorne Hotel. You can check out the beautiful fall foliage, and the hotel celebrates Halloween all month long. A special treat for those with a penchant for ghost stories: The Hawthorne's Family Fright Night is appropriate for all ages and features scary stories as well as milk and cookies. Small- to medium-sized dogs welcome. $10 fee per day.

(781) - Waltham

The Westin: Waltham-Boston

(781) 290-5600
70 3rd Ave
(@ Totten Pond Rd)
Waltham, Massachusetts 02451
www.starwood.com/westin/waltham

Price Range: $$$

A short hop from Logan Airport and a 15-minute drive from downtown, the Westin Waltham is a centerpiece of Boston's beltway. The hotel sits a mile from the corporate offices of IBM, Oracle and Microsoft. It's even closer to the dog park on Totten Pond Road, definitely the best place to take your pup for a stroll. The Waltham provides a dog bed and a bag of goodies at check-in. The hotel restaurant, Seventy @ Third, is known for its New England clam chowder. You may also want to check out the lobby bar, which offers sweeping views of the city's high-tech corridor. $100 deposit. No weight limit.

Michigan

(734) - Detroit

The Westin: Detroit Metropolitan Airport

(313) - Dearborn

The Ritz-Carlton: Dearborn

(248) - Southfield

The Westin: Southfield Detroit

(734) - Detroit

The Westin: Detroit Metropolitan Airport

(734) 942-6500
2501 Worldgateway Pl
(off John D Dingell Dr)
Detroit, Michigan 48242
www.starwood.com/westin/detroit
Price Range: $$$

Tranquility isn't typically the first word that pops to mind when one thinks of an airport, but this Westin at Midfield Terminal is serene. A Zen-like ambience resonates through its eight-story atrium. Bamboo trees and dark wood highlight the Eastern theme that carries over to its signature restaurant, Dema. If you feel like snapping out of the Zen zone, there's a state-of-the-art fitness center on site and you can tune into TVs at every exercise station. Dog amenities include the Westin's signature Heavenly Dog Bed. However, without any nearby parks, you're limited to the small walking area outside the hotel. No fee. 40-pound weight limit.

(313) - Dearborn

The Ritz-Carlton: Dearborn

(313) 441-2000
300 Town Center Dr
(between Hubbard Dr & Southfield Fwy)
Dearborn, Michigan 48126
www.ritzcarlton.com/hotels/dearborn
Price Range: $$$$$
A *Condé Nast* Gold List Reserve pick, the Ritz-Carlton
Dearborn sits on seven acres in the heart of chic Fairlane.
People perks include an indoor pool and 24-hour room service. The hotel's restaurant, the Grill, landed the Best
Restaurant honor (2003) and Top 10 Tables pick (2004) in
the *Detroit Free Press*. While you shop at nearby Fairlane Town
Center—Ritz Carlton guests get a VIP discount card—the hotel
will set you up with dog-walking and pet-sitting services.
When you're on dog-walking detail, take your pup for a stroll
past the Henry Ford—the largest indoor-outdoor museum in
the country. $150 fee. 50-pound weight limit.

(248) - Southfield

The Westin: Southfield Detroit

(248) 827-4000
1500 Town Center
(between Evergreen & Ten Mile rds)
Southfield, Michigan 48075
www.starwood.com/westin/southfield
Price Range: $$$
This Westin is attached to Southfield Town Center—a business,
financial and shopping Mecca. The hotel also sits near area
Fortune 500 companies, downtown and the Joe Louis Arena.
Though the nearest dog park is half a mile away, the hotel
grounds provide your pup plenty of room to play. People perks

include a fitness center, heated indoor pool and hot tub—the honeymoon suite also offers an in-room whirlpool. Dog amenities include a Heavenly Dog Bed, treats and a room-service menu with dog delicacies. No fee. 40-pound weight limit.

Minnesota

(612) - Minneapolis

Le Meridien: Minneapolis
The Marquette

(952) - Bloomington

Sofitel: Minneapolis

(612) - Minneapolis

Le Meridien: Minneapolis
(612) 677-1100
601 1st Ave N
(@ 6th St)
Minneapolis, Minnesota 55403
www.minneapolis.lemeridien.com
Price Range: $$$$
The best thing about this world-class luxury hotel is its location: Shopping, business and theater are all nearby. Loring Park, about 12 blocks away, offers dog-walking paths that wind around lakes and gardens, and the nearby Minneapolis Sculpture Garden is home to a wide range of outdoor art. Winter visitors take note: The city's average temperature drops well below zero, so come prepared. Although Le Meridien doesn't provide any additional amenities for pets, the staff will happily coordinate any pet services you may need. The all-white room decor has prompted a pricey pet fee of $150 per night. 35-pound weight limit.

The Marquette

(800) 328-4782
710 Marquette Ave
(@ 7th, in the IDS Bldg)
Minneapolis, Minnesota 55402
www.marquettehotel.com

Price Range: $$$$

The friendly service is legendary at this hotel, which caters to business travelers. The business center always has fresh coffee and freshly baked cookies. And the executive floor has its own lounge complete with a complimentary full bar. Guest perks include a 24-hour fitness center and access to the Litespa, plus the YMCA pool. The hotel is connected to the posh Nicollet Mall by skybridge to keep you warm as you wander in winter. $200 deposit. 35-pound weight limit.

(952) - Bloomington

Sofitel: Minneapolis

(952) 835-1900
5601 W 78th St
(@ Picture Dr)
Bloomington, Minnesota 55439
www.sofitel.com

Price Range: $$$

As a AAA four-diamond winner for 21 years running, this comfy business-centered Sofitel comes equipped with geometric inspired rooms, a gym and two restaurants. Chez Colette is a 1920s-style French brassiere, and La Fougasse offers Mediterranean dishes, an open-view kitchen and a fireplace. The hotel is close to both the Minneapolis airport and Lake Harriet, which offers canoeing, biking, hiking, concerts and plenty of grass to play Frisbee with your dog. The Sofitel is about a 10-minute drive from the Mall of America, where more than 500 shops, 50 restaurants and a handful of nightclubs are under one roof. No fee. 20-pound weight limit.

Missouri

(314) - Clayton, St. Louis

The Ritz-Carlton: St. Louis
The Westin: St. Louis

(816) - Kansas City

The Westin: Crown Center

(314) - Clayton, St. Louis

The Ritz-Carlton: St. Louis
(314) 863-6300
100 Carondelet Pl
(between Hanley Rd & Forsyth Blvd)
Clayton, Missouri 63105
www.ritzcarlton.com/hotels/st_louis
Price Range: $$$$$
Situated amid the fashionable Clayton business and shopping district, this Ritz, a *Condé Nast Traveler* Gold List honoree, is just minutes from a championship golf course, Saks Fifth Avenue and Nieman Marcus. For a good, long walk with your dog, Forest Park is two miles away. This dog haven, which was once home to the 1904 St. Louis World's Fair, is even bigger than Central Park and attracts 12 million visitors a year. The Ritz offers treats upon request. People perks include hydrotherapy pools, a steam room, sauna and fitness center, a cigar bar and private balconies in every room. There's a two-pet maximum and a $125 fee per stay. 50-pound weight limit.

The Westin: St. Louis
(314) 621-2000
811 Spruce St
(@ 9th St)
St. Louis, Missouri 63102
www.starwood.com/westin/stlouis
Price Range: $$$

Located in Cupples Station within view of the Gateway Arch, this Westin offers both city- and stadium-view rooms. The loft-like Clark Street Grill serves American cuisine, and you can watch your food being prepared in their all-in-view kitchen. Your pup is welcome in the grassy courtyard of the hotel or you can drive a couple of miles to the gigantic Forest Park: At 1,300 acres, it's a St. Louis landmark. No fee. 20-pound weight limit.

(816) - Kansas City

The Westin: Crown Center
(816) 474-4400
1 E Pershing Rd
(between Main St & Grand Blvd)
Kansas City, Missouri 64108
www.starwood.com/westin/crowncenter
Price Range: $$$

This Westin—complete with a five-story waterfall—is inside Hallmark's Crown Center, a Kansas City shopping, theater and restaurant landmark. The Westin boasts the rooftop steakhouse, Benton's, and offers tennis, a sauna, a steam room and a jog-ging track. Across the street, Bark Park offers three acres of off-leash, fenced-in running space inside Penn Valley Park. No fees if your dog is under 50 pounds. Otherwise $10 a night.

Nevada

(702) - Henderson, Las Vegas

Green Valley Ranch Resort and Spa
The Ritz-Carlton: Lake Las Vegas
Four Seasons Hotel: Las Vegas
The Westin: Casuarina Hotel & Spa

Four Seasons Hotel: Las Vegas

(702) 632-5000
3960 S Las Vegas Blvd
(@ Four Seasons Dr)
Las Vegas, Nevada 89119
www.fourseasons.com/lasvegas
Price Range: $$$$$
Very Vegas with glitz, gold and a bit of glamour, this Four
Seasons manages to toe the line between the Strip and a
renowned Mediterranean resort. You can't gamble at the hotel,
but you can enjoy a JAMU massage, get spritzed with Evian
water by the pool attendants, or get a chilled towel at the fitness center. The Bali Hai Golf Course is three minutes away.
Verandah, the resident restaurant serves Italian-inspired cuisine, and the Pool Bar serves drinks and salads. Your pup will
receive bowls and freshly baked biscuits, as well as complimentary walks on the Strip. Crate your pup when you leave
him in the room. No fee. 25-pound weight limit.

Green Valley Ranch Resort and Spa
(866) 782-9487
2300 Paseo Verdi Pkwy
(between Rt 215 & Griffin Valley Pkwy)
Henderson, Nevada 89052
www.greenvalleyranchresort.com
Price Range: $$$$
Only seven miles from the Las Vegas Strip, this resort and spa
offers serenity, as well as an on-site casino and complimentary
shuttle service to the Strip. Spa fanatics will appreciate the 20
different massage treatments. And guests will enjoy watching
hotel employees gather at dusk to light the hundreds of candles through the lobby area. Dancing at the hotel's night club,
the Whiskey, is also popular. Dog amenities include a mat,
dog biscuits, food and water bowls plus complimentary Fiji
water. $20 daily fee. 20-pound weight limit.

The Ritz-Carlton: Lake Las Vegas
(702) 567-4700
1610 Lake Las Vegas Pkwy
(@ Lake Mead Dr)
Henderson, Nevada 89011
www.ritzcarlton.com/resorts/lake_las_vegas/
Price Range: $$$$$
With a championship golf course, rated fifth in the country by
Condé Nast Traveler; an award-winning spa and fitness center;
plus sublime accommodations and gorgeous scenery; this
Ritz-Carlton offers a completely different experience then the
typical Vegas vacation. Small dogs are welcome but aren't permitted to walk around the hotel, even on leash. So keep him
in a tote or crate while you're on the property. Dog-friendly
areas include the Pet Walk and Lake Mead National
Recreation Area, the second-largest in the country. If you're in
the mood to gamble, take a shuttle to the Strip, just 17 miles
away. $150 per-pet fee. 25-pound weight limit.

The Westin: Casuarina Hotel & Spa

(702) 836-9775
160 E Flamingo Rd
(@ Koval Ln)
Las Vegas, Nevada 89109
www.starwood.com/westin/casuarina

Price Range: $$$$

If you think your dog is your lucky charm then take note: The casino at the Westin Casuarina lets your pup tag along (on leash) as you take on the slots, video poker or table games. Along with million-dollar jackpots, the hotel offers facials, massages, pedicures and manicures at the Hibiscus Spa, dry and wet saunas as well as an outdoor hot tub and pool—all off-limits to your pet. You can't leave your dog in the room alone unless she's crated so ask the concierge about pet-sitting services. No fee. 40-pound weight limit.

New Jersey

(609) - Princeton

The Westin: Princeton at Forrestal Village

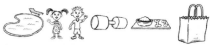

The Westin: Princeton at Forrestal Village

(609) 452-7900
201 Village Blvd
(@ Lionsgate Dr)
Princeton, New Jersey 08540
www.starwood.com/westin/princeton

Price Range: $$$

Only four miles from Princeton University, this Westin is located in Forrestal Village, an outlet shopper's haven. You have a choice of three hotel restaurants—including Bimi, a Japanese-style sushi bar where food is prepared tableside. You also have access to a pool, sauna, fitness facility, volleyball court and 10,000-square-foot ballroom that holds 1,600 guests. Your pup will enjoy the huge dog-walking area, as well as a running trail that begins a few blocks away. No fee. 40-pound weight limit.

New Mexico

(505) - Sante Fe

Ten Thousand Waves

Ten Thousand Waves

(505) 992-5025
3451 Hyde Park Rd
(@ La Entrada)
Santa Fe, New Mexico 87501
www.tenthousandwaves.com

Price Range: $$$$$

Adobe goes Eastern Zen at this hot springs resort and spa. Treatment options include 80-minute hot-stone massages, facials, scrubs, wraps, acupuncture and private hot tubs. Accommodations run from standard Zen-style rooms with no TV to the Emperor's Court, which includes a fireplace, deep tub and cable TV. Alas, your dog, though welcome, must be on leash when outside and on guard, since coyotes occasionally wander the property. The hotel also asks that your dog not be left alone in your room. $25 daily fee. No weight limit.

New York City

(212) – Manhattan

Upper East Side
The Carlyle
The Lowell
The Peninsula: New York
The Pierre
The Plaza Athenee
The Regency
The Sherry-Netherland Hotel
The Surrey

Upper West Side
Mandarin Oriental: New York
Phillips Club
The Ritz-Carlton: New York, Central Park
St. Regis Club at the Essex House
The Westin: Essex House on Central Park

Midtown
70 Park Avenue Hotel
Chambers Hotel
The Drake
Four Seasons Hotel: New York
Le Parker Meridian
The Muse
Paramount Hotel
RIHGA Royal
W: New York - Lexington
W: New York - The Court
W: New York - The Tuscany
W: New York - Times Square
W: New York - Union Square
The Westin: New York at Times Square
Sofitel: New York

Chelsea, South of 14th & SoHo
Maritime Hotel
The Ritz-Carlton: New York, Battery Park
SoHo Grand Hotel

Upper East Side

The Carlyle

(212) 744-1600
35 E 76th St (@ Madison Ave)
New York, New York 10021
www.thecarlyle.com

Price Range: $$$$$

This elegant, exquisitely appointed Rosewood hotel—the recipient of numerous awards from *Travel & Leisure* and *Condé Nast Traveler*—has catered to high society since 1930. From Truman to Reagan, many former presidents referred to the Carlyle as their home away from home. Luckily for your pup, they also cater to pets at no extra charge. Amenities include a dog bed and treats. And an eager staff member is always available to walk your dog. Its location on Madison Avenue gives pet owners immediate access to Central Park. The most sprawling green space in the city, it offers an abundance of room for your dog to roam and plenty of people watching. 25-pound weight limit.

The Lowell

(800) 745-8883
28 E 63rd St (@ Madison Ave)
New York, New York 10021
www.lhw.com/property.aspx?propertyid=332

Price Range: $$$$$

A member of the Leading Hotels of the World, the Lowell offers guests impeccable luxury accommodations and personal service on the city's exclusive Upper East Side. The Lowell is home to two restaurants: the formal Pembroke Room as well as the Post House, which offers more of a steakhouse atmosphere. The Lowell also provides your pup with outstanding service. Dog biscuits are always at the front desk, and room service will take a dog meal to your room daily: food and water bowls included. Dog-sitting services are also available. For $10, the hotel will take your pet to the ultimate pup playground, Central Park, a block-and-a-half away. No fee. No weight limit.

The Peninsula: New York

(800) 262-9467
700 5th Ave (@ 55th St)
New York, New York 10019
www.newyorkpeninsula.com
Price Range: $$$$

The velveteen sitting rooms, carved Mahogany tables and floor-to-ceiling city views at this turn-of-the-century hotel may make you wonder wether you've landed in an Edith Wharton novel. This AAA five-diamond hotel has received countless accolades from *Condé Nast Traveler*, *Travel & Leisure*, *Andrew Harper's Hideaway Report* and *New York* magazine, to name a few. Amenities abound, including high-speed Internet, a state-of-the-art fitness center with trainers, a steam room, sauna, pool, and award-winning spa. Fives, the hotel restaurant serves Atlantic Rim cuisine and the Pen-Top Bar & Terrace is quite the post-work corporate hot spot. Your pup will receive a bed and bowls at check in. No fee. 15-pound weight limit.

The Pierre

(212) 838-8000
E 61st St
(@ 5th Ave)
New York, New York 10021
www.fourseasons.com/pierre
Price Range: $$$$$

This 1930s landmark hotel—a permanent fixture on the *Condé Nast* Gold List—offers travelers exquisite European-style accommodations, superb service as well as modern conveniences. And it overlooks dog-friendly Central Park. Hand-painted murals and Italian marble adorn the 1,600-square-foot fitness center, and the spa services in this hotel include sublime massage and facial treatments. Afternoon tea in the Rotunda is also a highlight. Dog amenities include food dishes, a bed, bones and treats, and the concierge will arrange dog-care services. The hotel will provide maps of nearby jogging trails that double as dog-walking routes. No fee. 15-pound weight limit.

The Plaza Athenee
(800) 447-8800
37 E 64th St
(@ Madison Ave)
New York, New York 10021
www.plaza-athenee.com
Price Range: $$$$$

A regular on the *Condé Nast* Gold List, the Plaza Athenee is renowned for its luxe, European lodgings and superior service. It should come as no surprise that the hotel will go out of its way to accommodate any request you might have, especially those concerning your dog. Your pup stays free, and the staff will be happy to walk your dog or arrange pet services. Central Park, where you will find plenty of friendly dogs and like-minded people, is just steps away. The general manager's dog is usually around too, although he prefers to lounge in his suite. 25-pound weight limit.

The Regency
(212) 759-4100
540 Park Ave
(@ E 61st St)
New York, New York 10021
www.loewshotels.com/hotels/newyork/
Price Range: $$$$$

Offering outstanding services and amenities in an atmosphere of warm, understated, elegance, this luxury four-star hotel lives up to its Upper East Side, Park Avenue address. In keeping with Loews' pet-friendly policy, the dog perks are equally outstanding. The welcome package includes a signature pet bowl, placemat, toys and treats, as well as a personal note from the general manager, outlining hotel services as well as local pet-friendly resources, attractions and restaurants. The vet-approved pet room-service menu includes vegetarian alternatives. Their puppy pager enables the hotel staff to reach you should your dog need you while you're out. No fee. No weight limit.

The Sherry-Netherland Hotel

(800) 247-4377
781 5th Ave
(@ E 59th St)
New York, New York 10022
www.sherrynetherland.com

Price Range: $$$$$

Overlooking Central Park on fashionable Fifth Avenue, this residential hotel, which has been a New York landmark and status symbol since 1927, maintains its original character and charming service-oriented touches. All apartments, which are individually owned and decorated, must adhere to Sherry guidelines. The Netherland is perhaps best known for its efforts to preserve valuable pieces rescued from the Vanderbilt mansion, including grand chandeliers and an elegant marble floor. Pets of all sizes are welcome, free of charge, and the concierge stands at the ready with numbers for dog walkers and day-care facilities, as well as local vets and pet hospitals.

The Surrey

(212) 288-3700
20 E 76th St
(@ Madison Ave)
New York, New York 10021
www.affinia.com/6_10_sur_overview.cfm

Price Range: $$$$

This elegant Upper East Side hotel attends to the needs of all their guests, including dogs. The European-style rooms are quite comfortable, and the Jet Set Dog program includes a list of local resources, dog-friendly restaurants and dog runs, as well as a placemat, bowls, bones and other treats. Waste bags and stationery decorated with paw prints are complimentary. Alternative therapy aficionados might want to buy the Howlistic Travel Kit with therapeutic oils for dog massage. Guests also have access to two off-site Affinia spas. Central Park is just a few blocks away. Dogs stay free, but the hotel requires advance notice. No weight limit.

Upper West Side

Mandarin Oriental: New York
(212) 805 8800
80 Columbus Cir
(@ 60th St)
New York, New York 10023
www.mandarinoriental.com/newyork
Price Range: $$$$$
Part of an exclusive new development on floors 35 to 54 of the
Time Warner Center, the opulent Mandarin Oriental New York
boasts gorgeous views of the city's skyline. This Eastern hotel,
which is known for its superior service and sublime decor,
treats dogs exceptionally. After presenting your dog with a gift
basket full of treats and amenities, the concierge will help
schedule any dog-care services you may need. Central Park is
across the street and gives your pet ample room to run on or off
leash. At night, you'll find an orchid on your pillow, and your
dog will get a treat. No fee. No weight limit.

Phillips Club
(212) 835-8800
155 W 66th St
(between Broadway & Amsterdam Ave)
New York, New York 10023
www.phillipsclubnewyork.com
Price Range: $$$$$
The swanky Phillips Club—a part of the Millennium Partners
utopian urban complex on Lincoln Square—offers guests
exceptional hotel service in apartment-style studios and suites
that come complete with kitchenettes. Perks include privileges
at the exclusive Reebok Sports Club. Your dog will appreciate
the proximity to Central Park: It's practically your backyard.
The Phillips Club will connect you with dog-walking and sitting services. For other amenities, ask before arriving. No fee.
No weight limit.

The Ritz-Carlton: New York, Central Park

(212) 308-9100
50 Central Park South
(@ 59th St & 6th Ave)
New York, New York 10019
www.ritzcarlton.com/hotels/new_york_central_park
Price Range: $$$$$

The Central Park Ritz sets the bar for dog accoutrement. Not only do they provide beds, pillows, ID tags (gold plated no less) and rainproof dog gear—they have an entire package devoted to pups, aptly named Doggy & Me. There's plenty for you as well, including spa packages, shopping excursions, and, of course, Central Park is just outside your door. But you may never want to leave your room, which comes standard with a marble soaking tub, a flat screen television and high-speed Internet. Downstairs, Atelier restaurant serves up French fare, and the Star Lounge is a great place to grab a cocktail. No fee. 50-pound weight limit. Two-pet maximum.

St. Regis Club at the Essex House

(212) 247-0300
170 Central Park South
(@ 7th Ave)
New York, New York 10019
www.essexhouse.com
Price Range: $$$$$

Located at the southern perimeter of Central Park, the statuesque Essex House is the perfect starting place for an afternoon dog walk. The luxe St. Regis Club, making up the 19th through 39th floors of this historic building, promises amazing views from every room. The hotel boasts the five-star restaurant Alain Ducasse, which offers one of the best Sunday brunches in the city. Hotel offerings include a state-of-the-art business center, spa and fitness center. The St. Regis shares its building and front desk with the Westin, and provides your pup with Westin dog amenities: food and water bowls, floor mats and a Westin Heavenly Dog Bed. No fee. 40-pound weight limit.

The Westin: Essex House on Central Park

(212) 247-0300
160 Central Park South
(between 6th & 7th aves)
New York, New York 10019
www.starwood.com/westin/essexhouse

Price Range: $$$$

The Westin Essex House, which shares a lobby and front desk with the St. Regis Club, is right by Carnegie Hall and 5th Avenue. Both you and your pup will appreciate the close proximity to Central Park (one block), which offers nearly 850 acres. The hotel provides their signature Heavenly Dog Bed, toys and bowls. The concierge has details about walking and sitting services. Don't miss the weekend brunch at Cafe Botanica, which offers park-side views. No fee. 30-pound weight limit.

Midtown

70 Park Avenue Hotel

(877) 707-2752
70 Park Ave (@ 38th St)
New York, New York 10016
www.70thparkave.com

Price Range: $$$$

This hip Kimpton hotel offers you exceptional service, plush accommodations and a long list of amenities in a convenient midtown location. People perks include 24-hour in-room televised yoga instruction and the Kimpton's standard complimentary evening wine reception. You're within easy walking distance of Madison, Fifth Avenue, Rockefeller Center, Broadway and several museums. The hotel asks that you keep your dog crated when left alone in the room. However, the concierge will arrange dog-sitting or walking. Only a portion of the deluxe rooms in this hotel are pet-friendly, so be sure to tell them that you will be traveling with your dog. Small- and medium-sized dogs only. $100 deposit.

Chambers Hotel

(212) 974-5656
15 W 56th St
(between 5th & 6th aves)
New York, New York 10019
www.chambershotel.com

Price Range: $$$$$

Catering to the fashion and beauty industry's it crowd, this uber-chic hotel is located in the epicenter of the famed 5th Avenue shopping district. Chambers offers every amenity and service a fashionista could want—including a personal shopper and makeup artist from Henri Bendel, in-room personal training and yoga instruction, spa services courtesy of Mario Bedesku Skin Care as well as a car and driver. The Chambers is also home to current hot spot, Town, which offers French cuisine and a balcony lounge. The edgy SoHo loft-style guest rooms are infused with photography-quality lighting and perfectly chosen colors. And Central Park is a short stick's throw away. No fee. 20-pound weight limit.

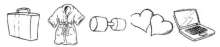

The Drake

(212) 421-0900
440 Park Ave
(@ 56th St)
New York, New York 10022
www.swissotel.com/ms-basics.asp?id=5

Price Range: $$$$

Located in the heart of Manhattan, the Drake lives up to its prestigious Park Avenue address. The staff is on hand for anything you might want, and like all the Raffles hotels, there are plenty of perks to take advantage of. You can indulge in the signature Park Avenue spa and fitness packages during your stay, where the pampering menu covers everything from hot stone therapy and skincare to luxurious body treatments. And Q56, the hotel's posh restaurant, is a great place for power lunches. The Drake is only five blocks from central park—perfect for an afternoon dog walk. No fee. No weight limit.

Four Seasons Hotel: New York

(212) 758-5700
57 E 57th St (between Madison & Park aves)
New York, New York 10022
www.fourseasons.com/newyorkfs
Price Range: $$$$$

Even among the superior Four Seasons hotels, this ideally located 57th Street hotel, designed by I.M. Pei, is a standout. Exquisitely appointed, plush guestrooms, offering every amenity you could want, are serene. The spa offerings are among the best you'll find in the city. Dog perks include a basket of dog treats upon arrival, Four Seasons water and food bowls as well as a sleeping pad. Please note that the hotel prefers dogs not be left in the room unattended and offers pet-sitting for $20 an hour with a four-hour minimum. The hotel also offers dog walks in Central Park for $10. No fee. 15-pound weight limit.

Le Parker Meridian

(800) 543-4300
119 W 56th St (between 6th & 7th aves)
New York, New York 10019
www.parkermeridien.com/main.html
Price Range: $$$$$

This park-side hotel offers an extraordinary list of amenities and services: The business center has everything from computers to cell phones, plus messenger service and secretarial support. The on-site fitness center, Gravity, offers racquetball and basketball courts, as well as strength-training and cardio equipment. The Meridian also boasts an indoor pool. Other offerings include a holistic spa, nutrition counseling and personal training. Dining options include the wildly popular, enticingly inexpensive Burger Bar, as well as the decadent Norma's for breakfast—where the starter meal for two can run a tab into the $80 range. Dog amenities include a room-service menu and dog walking. No weight limit. A cleaning fee is charged only when necessary.

The Muse

(877) 692-6873
130 W 46th St
(between 6th & 7th aves)
New York, New York 10036
www.themusehotel.com

Price Range: $$$$

Inspiration by design is, quite appropriately, the theme at the Muse, which offers top-of-the-line accommodations in an environment that is the perfect combination of creativity and comfort. The 15-foot vaulted ceiling with a mural of nine muses is best regarded from one of the lobby's supremely comfortable velvet chairs. The hotel offers the District for dining and the Mini-Bar (no, not the one in your room) for cocktails. It's an easy walk to Broadway, Times Square and Rockefeller Center. No weight limit or fee, but the amenities are on you.

Paramount Hotel

(212) 764-5500
235 W 46th St
(@ 8th Ave)
New York, New York 10036
www.paramount-hotel.net411.com

Price Range: $$$$

The rooms may be small, but service is huge at the perennially hip Paramount Hotel. Hipsters love the Whiskey Bar, while quieter types appreciate the coziness of the upstairs Library, which doubles as a restaurant and bar. Other perks include a newsstand in the lobby and the Dean & Deluca coffee shop. The Paramount is discriminating about the dogs they welcome: Management gives approval on a case-by-case basis, and all arrangements must be made before arrival. But one thing is for sure: the smaller the dog, the better. You can't leave your pet in the room alone. Central Park is a bit of a hike but also a great place to take your dog.

RIHGA Royal
(866) 656-1777
151 W 54th St
(between 6th & 7th aves)
New York, New York 10019
www.rihgaroyalny.com
Price Range: $$$$$
The RIHGA offers an ideal midtown location close to cultural attractions, upscale restaurants, world-class shopping and unparalleled people watching. The RIHGA Royal staff is especially helpful. And you don't even have to leave your suite for a workout. No less than 500 square feet, the suites are equipped with a Bowflex strength machine as well as other exercise accessories. Exercise equipment not withstanding, the decor is old-school elegant meets serene minimalism. Your small dog stays free, but you're expected to carry her through the lobby. 10-pound weight limit.

Sofitel: New York
(212) 354-8844
45 W 44th St
(between 5th & 6th sts)
New York, New York 10036
www.sofitel.com
Price Range: $$$
This Sofitel is close to many popular New York landmarks—including Carnegie Hall, Rockefeller Center, MOMA, all of the Broadway theaters, and of course, Times Square. The hotel's comfy art-deco rooms provide plenty of room to relax. A fitness center is on-site as well as Gaby—the resident French-Asian fusion restaurant. Bryant Park is nearby and perfect for some on-leash strolling. Or you can always head to Central Park with your pup. No fee. No weight limit.

W: New York – Lexington

(212) 755-1200
541 Lexington Ave
(@ E 49th St)
New York, New York 10022
www.starwood.com/whotels/newyork

Price Range: $$$$

The first hotel in the W chain, the W's Lexington outpost is a haven for people and their pets. You can wander through the nearby UN Plaza Park, socialize in Central Park's dog run or stroll down Madison Avenue. Amenities include a welcome package (toy, gourmet treat, W Hotel pet tag and cleanup bags), in-room dog necessities (pet bed, food and water bowls, Pet in Room sign, turndown treat) and essential pet-service referrals (pet-sitting, dog-walking, vet, grooming, specialty stores). Room service will bring anything you forgot, from leashes and toys to food and treats. $25 a night, with a $100 cleaning fee. No weight limit.

W: New York – The Court

(212) 685-1100
130 E 39th St
(@ Lexington Ave)
New York, New York 10016
www.starwood.com/whotels/thecourt

Price Range: $$$$

The decor is of this hotel is W-style residential, meaning the avant-garde design is exceedingly comfortable. Situated between Lexington and Park avenues in one of Midtown's oldest neighborhoods, this W hotel is surrounded by tree-lined streets, a rarity in Manhattan. Dog amenities include the standard W welcome package (toy, gourmet treat, W Hotel pet tag, cleanup bags), in-room dog necessities (pet bed, food and water bowls, Pet in Room sign, turn-down treat) and essential service referrals. Room service will bring anything you forgot, from leashes and toys to food and treats. $25 a night, plus a $100 cleaning fee. 50-pound weight limit.

W: New York - The Tuscany

(212) 686-1600
120 E 39th St
(@ Lexington Ave)
New York, New York 10016
www.starwood.com/whotels/thetuscany

Price Range: $$$$

If you're traveling by train, it's tough to beat the convenience of this Grand Central Station-adjacent W hotel that has the feel of an upscale European cafe. And with Rande Gerber's hipster hangout Cherry on the premises, you don't have to leave to find the scene. Also on-site is the W Cafe, a fitness center and spa services. Dog amenities include the standard W welcome package (toy, gourmet treat, W Hotel pet tag, cleanup bags), in-room dog necessities (pet bed, food and water bowls, Pet in Room sign and turndown treat), and essential service referrals. $25 a night, plus a $100 cleaning fee. No weight limit.

W: New York - Times Square

(212) 930-7400
1567 Broadway
(@ 47th St)
New York, New York 10036
www.starwood.com/whotels/timessquare

Price Range: $$$$$

On the *Condé Nast Traveler* Hot List of Hotels, the Times Square W is a Zen-like paradise for travelers and their pups. Nearby dog offerings include upscale pet boutiques, Chelsea Waterside and DeWitt Clinton parks as well as Bonnie's K9 Swim Center. Amenities include the standard welcome package (toy, gourmet treat, W Hotel pet tag, cleanup bags), in-room dog necessities and essential service referrals. Room service will bring anything you forgot, from leashes and toys to food and treats. Pet rates are $25 a night, plus a $100 cleaning fee. No weight limit.

W: New York – Union Square

(212) 253-9119
201 S Park Avenue
(@ E 17th St)
New York, New York 10003
www.starwood.com/whotels/unionsquare

Price Range: $$$$

The David Rockwell-designed, candle-lit Union Square W, is a *Condé Nast Traveler* Gold List Reserve pick. The W is also home to Rande Gerber's uber-hip Underbar as well as Todd English's restaurant, Olives. After a day at Union Square Park, your pup can enjoy a relaxing dog massage and order a sirloin steak from the pets-only menu. Amenities include the standard W welcome package (toy, gourmet treat, W Hotel pet tag, cleanup bags), in-room dog necessities (pet bed, food and water bowls, Pet in Room sign and turndown treat) and essential service referrals. $25 a night, plus a $100 cleaning fee. 25-pound weight limit.

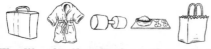

The Westin: New York at Times Square

(212) 201-2700
270 W 43rd Ave
(between 7th & 8th aves)
New York, New York 10036
www.starwood.com/westin/timessquare

Price Range: $$$$

This 45-story prism-skyscraper towers over glitzy Times Square, the ultimate shopping, dining and entertainment extravaganza. Forty theaters on Broadway are within walking distance. The concierge will set up your pup's appointments, including meal deliveries, grooming, dog walking and pet-sitting or even manicures and pedicures with round-trip limo service. But if you prefer to stay in, the Westin boasts a fitness center, full-service spa and Shula's steakhouse. No fee. No weight limit.

Chelsea, South of 14th & SoHo

Maritime Hotel
(212) 242-4300
363 W 16th St (@ 9th Ave)
New York, New York 10011
www.themaritimehotel.com
Price Range: $$$$$

Tucked in Chelsea, among the avant-garde art galleries, the Maritime is truly a hidden gem. The decor toes the line between vintage-chic and Zen, and the accommodating staff is on hand to provide you with anything you may need, from reservations to recommendations for dog walkers and sitters. With restaurants such as the Biltmore Room and hot spots like the Open lounge in the vicinity, you won't be wanting for nightlife options. However, you may want to stay in because the rooms come with flat-screen TVs and high-speed Internet access. The hotel frowns on leaving your pup alone in the room. If you do—be sure to crate him. No fee. No weight limit.

The Ritz-Carlton: New York, Battery Park
(212) 344-0800
2 West St (@ Battery Pl)
New York, New York 10004
www.ritzcarlton.com/hotels/new_york_battery_park
Price Range: $$$$$

It's no surprise that this waterfront Ritz, with telescopes in all harbor-view rooms, landed on the coveted *Condé Nast Traveler* Hot List. The hotel boasts an award-winning French master chef, and other outstanding amenities and services include a full-service spa and bath butler. The hotel is by the Esplanade, a dog-friendly pedestrian paradise that runs through Battery Park City. Expect a lot of stopping for dog socialization, but be sure to make your way along the Hudson to see the Statue of Liberty, Ellis Island and the New Jersey coastline. Dog bowls and treats are provided, but no meals. $75 fee per pet. 20-pound weight limit.

SoHo Grand Hotel

(800) 965-3000
310 W Broadway
(between Grand & Canal sts)
New York, New York   10013
www.sohogrand.com

Price Range: $$$$$

This hotel, situated in fashionable SoHo, caters primarily to business travelers and movie-mogul types. Eclectic touches, such as the dominos-patterned steps to the lobby, add flair to the elegant timeless design. The eight-foot windows in the guestrooms offer mesmerizing views of the city. Dog offerings include food and water bowls, pet treats and a cushy bed. Dogs can be left in the room alone if they're crated. Otherwise, your pup is welcome to join you in the exquisite living room-style lounge. For exercise, head over to the West Side Highway for an on-leash jog or visit the small off-leash dog run in Washington Square Park. No fee. No weight limit.

New York State

(631) – Greenport

Greenporter Hotel and Spa

(518) – Lake Placid & Saranac Lake

Lake Placid Lodge
The Point: Saranac Lake

(631) – Greenport

Greenporter Hotel and Spa
(631) 477-0066
326 Front St (4th Ave)
Greenport, New York 11944
www.thegreenporter.com
Price Range: $$$$
This Long Island hotel and spa offers heavenly in-room holistic spa treatments, ranging from body-elixir and massage combination treatments to aromatherapy and herbalism in their well-appointed, minimalist, modern rooms. The Greenporter's restaurant, Cuvee, has been praised in *The New York Times* as well as *Wine Spectator* for its country French fare. The Long Island Railroad Station, historic Greenport village and 25 wineries are all close by. Pets are not to be left in the room unattended, so plan to take your dog with you or get a dog-sitter. The hotel offers a list of pet-care services, including walking and grooming. Advance notice is required. $50 fee, plus a $100 deposit. No big dogs.

(518) - Lake Placid & Saranac Lake

Lake Placid Lodge
(877) 523-2700
Whiteface Inn Rd
P.O. Box 550
(@ the Whiteface Inn Rd Loop)
Lake Placid, New York 12946
www.lakeplacidlodge.com
Price Range: $$$$$

Enjoy a romantic getaway for three—you, your significant other and your dog—at this luxury Relais & Chateaux lodge. Wood-burning fireplaces and deep-seat tubs for two are featured in all cabins, and a full Adirondack breakfast and afternoon high tea are included in the daily rate. $75 a night covers your dog's meals, bedding, treats, toys and anything else he might need. Hiking trails surround the property and skirt the Lake Placid peninsula. On cold, snowy nights, you may appreciate the covered walkway that connects all 17 cabins. Dogs are welcome on all areas of the property but must be leashed at all times. No weight limit.

The Point: Saranac Lake
(800) 255-3530
Directions are sent only after full prepayment is received
Saranac Lake, New York 12983
www.thepointresort.com
Price Range: $$$$$

This five-star Relais & Chateaux inn—once a Rockefeller vacation hideaway—with unparalleled service, accommodations and cuisine is considered one of the finest hotels in the world. Each of the 11 grand log-cabin guestrooms comes complete with a custom-made bed, supremely comfortable furnishings and a fireplace. Depending on the season, activities include horseback riding, fishing, ice fishing, boating, golfing, swimming, snow shoeing and ice skating. Although guests must be over 18, dogs are welcome, and your pup has free run of the resort. Dog amenities include a bed, food dishes and nightly turn-down service with treats and leftovers from the dining room. P.S. Room rates here start at $1,250, but dogs stay free. No weight limit.

North Carolina

(919) - Chapel Hill

Siena Hotel

(704) - Charlotte

The Westin: Charlotte

(919) - Chapel Hill

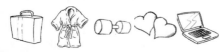

Siena Hotel
(800) 223-7379
1505 E Franklin St
(@ Estes Dr)
Chapel Hill, North Carolina 27514
www.sienahotel.com
Price Range: $$$$

The boutique Siena Hotel combines European elegance with Southern hospitality. Hotel offerings include Il Palio, the only AAA four-diamond restaurant in North Carolina, as well as a spa and fitness center. The award-winning UNC Finley golf course is four miles away, and guests receive preferred rates. This hotel is quite popular on parents' weekends, so check your schedule and call ahead. If your plans exclude your dog, Siena allows you to leave your dog alone in the room, as long as you leave a cell number with the front desk in case your pup gets fussy. $75 charge for dogs up to 50 pounds. $150 for dogs over 50 pounds.

(704) - Charlotte

The Westin: Charlotte

(704) 375-2600
601 S College St
(@ E Stonewall St)
Charlotte, North Carolina 28202
www.starwood.com/westin/charlotte

Price Range: $$$

There aren't many green patches in this part of Charlotte, but your pup is in luck. A little park is just steps away from this Westin. And if you feel like sightseeing, you can hop a trolley to the historic South End. Hotel offerings include a sauna, heated lap pool and state-of-the-art fitness facility, as well as the hotel's funky Bar 10. The Westin will provide your pup with a Heavenly Dog Bed, bowls and treats. The hotel asks that you crate your dog when he's left in the room alone. No fee. 50-pound weight limit.

Ohio

(614) – Columbus

The Westin: Columbus

(513) – Cincinnati

The Westin: Cincinnati

(216) – Cleveland

The Ritz-Carlton: Cleveland

(614) – Columbus

The Westin: Columbus

(614) 228-3800
310 S High St
(@ Main St)
Columbus, Ohio 43215
www.starwood.com/westin/columbus
Price Range: $$$

This elegant Westin Hotel, also known as the Great Southern Hotel, dates back to 1897. The landmark brick building boasts a magnificent three-story lobby, topped off by skylights. The quaint Victorian rooms, complete with cherry wood furnishings, vaulted ceilings and marble baths, are equipped with such modern conveniences as wireless Internet access. Nearby recreational offerings include golf, tennis and swimming, as well as walking/running trails for you and your dog. The closest, just two blocks away, leads down to the Scioto River. The famed, dog-friendly Schiller Park is two miles away. No fee. No weight limit.

(513) - Cincinnati

The Westin: Cincinnati

(513) 621-7700
21 E 5th St
(@ Vine St)
Cincinnati, Ohio 45202
www.starwood.com/westin/cincinnati

Price Range: $$$

Close to the Ohio River, this downtown Westin—complete
with a 24-hour on-site Kinko's—is tailored to business travel-
ers. Dogs fare well here too: The Doggie Welcome Kit comes
equipped with a Heavenly Dog Bed, bowls, placemat and ID.
Baggies are available for trips to Sawyer Point, a dog-friendly
park a half a mile away. The Tower Place Mall is connected to
the hotel by skybridge. Cincinnati's sports and entertainment
arenas are within walking distance. Hotel offerings include the
hotel restaurant serving heartland cuisine, an indoor pool, fit-
ness center and a sports bar. The hotel asks that you crate your
dog if she's alone in the room. No fee. 40-pound weight limit.

(216) - Cleveland

The Ritz-Carlton: Cleveland

(216) 623-1300
1515 W 3rd St
(@ Prospect Ave)
Cleveland, Ohio 44113
www.ritzcarlton.com/hotels/cleveland

Price Range: $$$$$

The city's only four-star hotel, the Cleveland Ritz was picked
for both *Travel & Leisure's* 100 Best Hotels list and the *Condé
Nast Traveler* Gold List. Package options include Rockin' at the
Ritz Carlton, which includes Rock & Roll Hall of Fame tickets,
and the Enchanted Evening: A romance package that includes

champagne, chocolate and rose petals scattered over your bed. The hotel is next to the Avenue at Tower City and within walking distance of Cleveland's theaters, the Rock & Roll Hall of Fame, the Gund Arena and Jacob's Field. Nearby Lake Erie (Lake of the Cat) is a fun place to explore with your pup. $50 fee per day. No weight limit.

Oklahoma

(405) – Oklahoma City

The Westin: Oklahoma City

The Westin: Oklahoma City

(405) 235-2780
1 N Broadway Cir
(@ N Broadway Dr)
Oklahoma City, Oklahoma 73102
www.starwood.com/westin/oklahomacity
Price Range: $$$
There's no end to the dog-walking possibilities near this Westin.
The free outdoor Myriad Botanical Gardens are a block away,
and Bricktown—the colorful, revitalized commercial district—
is even closer. There's also the underground tunnel, a city
beneath the city, which connects virtually all downtown build-
ings, but unless your pup fits in your bag, he isn't welcome.
The Westin boasts the Aria Grill which features High Plains
specialties, such as Flaming Raspberry Duck. Dog amenities
include a Westin Heavenly Dog Bed. No fee. No weight limit.

Oregon

(541) – Gleneden Beach & Hood River

Salishan Lodge & Golf Resort
Columbia Gorge Hotel

(503) – Portland

5th Avenue Suites
The Heathman Hotel
Hotel Vintage Plaza
RiverPlace Hotel
The Westin: Portland

(541) – Gleneden Beach & Hood River

Salishan Lodge & Golf Resort

(888) 725-4742
7760 Highway 101 North (between Hwys 18 & 20)
Gleneden Beach, Oregon 97388
www.salishan.com
Price Range: $$$$

Recently remodeled, the Salishan Spa & Golf Resort is an absolutely stunning beachside retreat on the Oregon coastline. They hosted their first official dog event, a Portuguese water dog trial, in October 2004 and hope to host more soon. The hotel welcomes your pup with treats and will direct you to the beach just across the highway, where well-trained dogs are free to play off leash. Barking dogs are not permitted to stay in your room unattended. However, many dog-friendly open spaces make it easy to take your pup with you wherever you go. $25 fee. No weight limit.

Columbia Gorge Hotel

(800) 345-1921
4000 Westcliff Dr (off Hwy 84)
Hood River, Oregon 97031
www.columbiagorgehotel.com

Price Range: $$$$

This quaint hotel offers plenty of personal touches, including turn-down service with chocolate and a rose, as well as champagne and caviar in the afternoon. Upon arrival, dog guests are greeted by Tux, the resident dog, and given a treat-filled doggie bowl. Although your pup can't stay in the room unattended, the staff will walk him for you. Check out the extensive grounds or nearby park: Both have tempting cliffs to explore but should be done so on leash. For off-leash adventure, head to the Columbia Gorge River. Nearby activities include skiing, golf, wind surfing or simply taking in the unbelievable scenery. $25 per night fee. No weight limit.

(503) - Portland

5th Avenue Suites

(888) 207-2201
506 SW Washington St (@ 5th Ave)
Portland, Oregon 97204
www.5thavenuesuites.com

Price Range: $$$

A pick for *Travel & Leisure's* Top 500 Hotels and the *Condé Nast Traveler* Gold List, this elegant hotel sits in a 1912 building—once home to the Lipman Wolfe department store. The guestrooms, done in shades of gold, are as comfortable as they are elegant. Dog amenities include bowls, treats and a copy of *Dog Nose News*, which lists dog-friendly restaurants, attractions and walking trails. If you're here on the last Friday of the month, get a reading from pet psychic Faye Petrowski during the hotel's wine hour, or you can pick up a paintbrush and canvas and do a little painting as you sip your wine. No fee. No weight limit.

The Heathman Hotel

(800) 551-0011
1001 SW Broadway (@ Salmon St)
Portland, Oregon 97205
www.heathmanhotel.com

Price Range: $$$$

Located in downtown Portland, the Heathman—recently
named as one of *Travel & Leisure's* Top 100 Hotels in the
country—has the comforts of home, plus nightly turn-down
service; a library, complete with librarian; as well as 400 films.
Room options include a unique parlor room with a pull-down
bed. All rooms come with a fully stocked bar. Directories feature a running map, which doubles nicely as a dog-walking
guide. Other hotel perks include a fitness center and an
award-winning restaurant serving Pacific Northwest cuisine
with a French flair. The hotel's Marble Bar offers cocktails, dining and jazz. $25 fee. 50-pound weight limit.

Hotel Vintage Plaza

(800) 263-2305
422 SW Broadway (between Washington & Stark sts)
Portland, Oregon 97205
www.vintageplaza.com

Price Range: $$$

A *Travel & Leisure* Top 500 Hotels in the World pick, the
Vintage Plaza, with its vineyard-inspired decor, is as comfort-
able as it is chic. Rooms run from the plenty plush to the two-
story suites that include a Japanese tub for two. People perks
include the complimentary evening wine hour in the hotel
lobby. Your dog receives a mat, complimentary bowls, rawhide
treat, bottled water and a pooper-scooper. This Kimpton hotel
will also provide information on the best spots for walking, as
well as dog-friendly restaurants and attractions in the area.
There are no additional fees for dog guests, and both dog
walking and pet-sitting are complimentary. No weight limit.

RiverPlace Hotel
(800) 227-1333
1510 SW Harbor Way
(@ Montgomery St)
Portland, Oregon 97201
www.riverplacehotel.com
Price Range: $$$$$

Oregon's only luxury waterfront resort, the RiverPlace Hotel overlooks the marina and is close to shopping, nightclubs and fine restaurants. Despite its downtown Portland location, the hotel offers fantastic roaming for you and your pup: walk along the Willamette River, enjoy leashed play in the adjacent park or take a 10-minute car ride to the off-leash parks at Washington Park or Mount Taber. Give the hotel advance notice, and you'll find a personalized bowl and biscuit waiting. All rooms require a $45 post-pet cleaning fee. No size limit for guestrooms, but the adjacent residential suites have a 30-pound weight limit.

The Westin: Portland
(503) 294-9000
750 SW Alder St
(between Park Ave & Broadway)
Portland, Oregon 97205
www.starwood.com/westin/portland
Price Range: $$$

This four-star hotel is right in the middle of downtown Portland, close to shopping, museums, golf courses and casinos. You're also a short drive from the Willamette River waterfront, frequented by walkers, joggers and dog lovers. There are two small but grassy on-leash parks within walking distance of the hotel. Dog amenities include the signature Heavenly Dog Bed and bowls. The hotel asks that you not leave your dog in the room unattended. So you may want to get a pet-sitter and check out the chicken pot-pie at the Daily Grill. Or there's always room service. No fee. 100-pound weight limit.

Pennsylvania

(215) - Philadelphia

Four Seasons Hotel: Philadelphia
Rittenhouse Hotel
The Rittenhouse Hotel
The Ritz-Carlton: Philadelphia
Sofitel: Philadelphia
The Westin: Philadelphia

(412) - Pittsburgh

The Westin: Convention Center Pittsburgh

(814) - Bradford

Glendorn

(215) - Philadelphia

Four Seasons Hotel: Philadelphia
(215) 963-1500
1 Logan Sq
(off Logan Cir)
Philadelphia, Pennsylvania 19103
www.fourseasons.com/philadelphia
Price Range: $$$$$
The Philadelphia Four Seasons embodies the luxury and elegance this chain is known for with Federal-era decor reflecting this region's history. The Four Seasons provides dogs with treats on arrival, plus a room service menu just for pets. The hotel staff will also take your pup for a walk at Swan Fountain. The Four Seasons doesn't allow dogs to stay in the room unattended, so plan to take your dog with you or prepare to pay a dogsitter $25 per hour with a three-hour minimum. Dogs stay free. 15-pound weight limit.

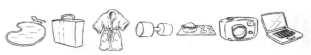

Rittenhouse Hotel

(800) 635-1042
210 W Rittenhouse Sq
(between 19th & Walnut sts)
Philadelphia, Pennsylvania 19103
www.rittenhousehotel.com

Price Range: $$$$$

Always one of *Condé Nast's* and *Travel & Leisure's* best-hotel picks, this luxe five-star hotel is reason enough to visit Philadelphia. Hosting the award-winning restaurant, Lacroix, a full service spa and salon and a state-of-the-art fitness center, the Rittenhouse is a great place for a romantic vacation or just a quick get away. The hotel's exceptional customer service extends to pups, offering snacks and a relaxing dog CD at check-in, plus dog-care arrangements. The on-leash Rittenhouse Park is across the street. For off-leash play, the enormous Fairmount Park is a 10-minute drive away, and Schuykill River is a few minutes closer. No fee. No weight limit.

The Ritz-Carlton: Philadelphia

(215) 523-8000
10 Avenue of the Arts
(@ Chestnut St)
Philadelphia, Pennsylvania 19102
www.ritzcarlton.com/hotels/philadelphia

Price Range: $$$$$

A spectacular city landmark resembling the Pantheon in Rome, the Philadelphia Ritz is grand even by Ritz-Carlton standards. Dining offerings include breakfast at the Pantheon, tea at the Rotunda and dinner at the Grill. The hotel has basic treats for your dog, but they're of the bag-and-can variety. People perks include a technology butler, a bath butler and a bath menu as well as a spa and fitness center and nearby golf courses. The hotel is a short walk from the Pennsylvania Convention Center, the Kimmel Center for the Performing Arts and Rittenhouse Square—a dog-friendly, on-leash park. $75 per day fee. No weight limit.

Sofitel: Philadelphia

(215) 569-8300
120 S 17th St
(@ Sansom St)
Philadelphia, Pennsylvania 19103
www.sofitel.com

Price Range: $$$

You won't find much in the way of dog offerings at this Sofitel, located in the heart of the business district. But the hotel does allow pets under 20 pounds for a nonrefundable $50 fee, and the soft-colored plush rooms are plenty big enough for you and your pup. A huge park about three blocks away provides the perfect place to give your dog some fresh air and exercise. Also within walking distance is the Liberty Bell and Independence Hall.

The Westin: Philadelphia

(215) 563-1600
99 S 17th St
(@ Chestnut St)
Philadelphia, Pennsylvania 19103
www.starwood.com/westin/philadelphia

Price Range: $$$

This magnificent Westin—bracketed by historical monuments, great shopping, a convention center and the Philadelphia Museum of Art—caters to both business and leisure travelers. This hotel was originally owned by Ritz Carlton, which is reflected in the grandness of the design and decor. Pet amenities include a Heavenly Dog Bed and bowls. People perks include the super comfy Westin signature Heavenly Bed, high-speed Internet access, plus a fitness center and sauna. The hotel also boasts the Grill Restaurant and Bar, as well as the Lobby Lounge. No fee. 40-pound weight limit.

(412) - Pittsburgh

The Westin: Convention Center Pittsburgh
(412) 281-3700
1000 Penn Ave
(10th St)
Pittsburgh, Pennsylvania 15222
www.starwood.com/westin/pittsburgh
Price Range: $$$
This Westin houses Pittsburgh's acclaimed Original Fish
Market featuring a sushi bar, daily menu and seaside decor.
And for business travelers, the Lawrence Convention Center
sits a block way. Though the nearest dog park is a bit farther,
picturesque Point State Park is worth the 10-block walk. The
National Historic Landmark on the riverfront also offers grassy
greens, city views and the Fort Pitt Museum. The Westin boasts
one of the top fitness centers in the state, equipped with
8,000-square-feet of free weights, aerobics and an indoor
lap pool. Post workout, relax with a steam, sauna or massage.
$50 fee. 25-pound weight limit.

(814) - Bradford

Glendorn
(800) 843-8568
1000 Glendorn Dr
(@ Corydon St)
Bradford, Pennsylvania 16701
www.glendorn.com
Price Range: $$$$$
The rustic accommodations at this Relais & Chateaux private
estate are infused with such luxurious touches that you may
never want to leave. Activities include swimming in the 80-
degree, 60-foot pool or hitting the trails on bicycle, snow-
shoes, cross-country skis or foot. You also may want to make a

selection from the Glendorn wine cellar, which includes more than 600 bottles. Pups are welcome everywhere, except the main house, and the Glendorn asks that dogs stay out of the lake. $75 per night. No weight limit.

Rhode Island

(401) - Providence

The Westin: Providence

The Westin: Providence
(401) 598-8000
1 W Exchange St
(@ Fountain St)
Providence, Rhode Island 29030
www.westinprovidence.com
Price Range: $$$
You can't miss the red brick tower of this grand four-star hotel, with a decor that is elegant without being ornate. Dining options include the casual International Yacht and Athletic Club, the fancier Agora Restaurant and the more intimate Library Bar and Lounge. The Westin offers a full-service business center, a fitness center and a heated indoor pool. The hotel connects to Providence Place Mall as well as the Rhode Island Convention Center. Across the street, the Riverwalk leads to Waterplace Park, which provides plenty of space and dog fraternization. Your dog receives biscuits and the Westin signature Heavenly Dog Bed. No fee. 40-pound weight limit.

South Carolina

(843) - Charleston

Charleston Place
The Westin Resort: Hilton Head Island

(803) - Aiken

The Willcox

(843) - Charleston

Charleston Place
(800) 611-5545
205 Meeting St
(@ Market St)
Charleston, South Carolina 29401
www.charlestonplace.com
Price Range: $$$$$
Surrounded by narrow cobblestone streets, horse-drawn car-
riages and spectacular antebellum homes, this exquisite Orient
Express hotel—a sister hotel of the Cipriani in Venice—
embodies old-world charm. Modern amenities include a full-
service European spa that offers every pampering therapeutic
treatment imaginable, plus Lollipop Manicures for kids. Pet
amenities, which include a special treat and a VIP package,
are equally pleasing. When your dog wants to play, take a
short walk to Ansonborough Field or Waterfront Park on the
Cooper River: Both spots are on-leash. Charleston is home to
two of the *Golf* magazine's 100 Best Golf Courses. $75 nightly
fee. No weight limit.

The Westin Resort: Hilton Head Island

(843) 681-4000
2 Grasslawn Ave (@ Folly Field Rd)
Hilton Head Island, South Carolina 29928
www.starwood.com/westin/hiltonhead
Price Range: $$$$

The Hilton Head Island Westin, attractive in its own right, is even more striking thanks to its location on a scenic stretch of white sandy beach. Each suite has a private balcony and Westin signature Heavenly Bed. You can ride bicycles on the beach or go for a dip in the Atlantic. But your pup is only allowed on the sand after 5 p.m. and only in the off-season, so make sure he's leashed and bring baggies. With the exception of the pool and the restaurant, dogs have free run of the grounds. For a fee the staff will provide a Westin Heavenly Dog Bed, leash, collar, bowls and meals. $100 fee. 40-pound weight limit.

(803) – Aiken

The Willcox

(877) 648-2200
100 Colleton Ave (@ Chesterfield St)
Aiken, South Carolina 29801
www.thewillcox.com
Price Range: $$$$

With grand columns, relaxing porches and ambling shady roads, the Willcox tips its hat to old-fashioned Southern charm. Extraordinary amenities include in-room fireplaces and a sublime spa. The hotel is closed for the summer from June 14 through Sept. 15. But spring is the time to visit, when the annual Aiken Triple Crown race—the town's see-and-be-seen event—takes place. People, Corgis and Jack Russells get decked out in their finest Burberry to catch a view of the thoroughbreds trotting to the starting gate. Scenic Hitchcock Woods, one of America's largest city parks, is a stick's throw away. Dogs are allowed at the Willcox on a limited basis. $50 fee. $200 deposit. No weight limit.

Texas

(512) – Austin

The Driskill
Four Seasons Hotel: Austin

(214) – Dallas

Hotel Crescent Court
Mansion on Turtle Creek
The Westin: City Center Dallas

(972) – Dallas, Frisco, Irving

The Westin: Galleria Dallas
The Westin: Park Central
The Westin: Stonebriar Resort
Four Seasons Resort and Club: Dallas - Las Colinas

(817) – Fort Worth

The Ashton

(713) – Houston

Four Seasons Hotel: Houston
The Lancaster Hotel
St. Regis: Houston
The Westin: Galleria Houston
The Westin: Oaks

(281) – Houston

Sofitel: Houston

(210) – San Antonio

La Mansion del Rio
The Westin Riverwalk

(512) - Austin

The Driskill
(800) 252-9367
604 Brazos St (@ E 6th St)
Austin, Texas 78701
www.driskillhotel.com
Price Range: $$$$

It's easy to forget you're in the heart of Austin's business and entertainment district when you walk into this century-old Romanesque hotel that features hand-painted ceilings and a stained-glass dome in the lobby. The elegant decor carries over into the Victorian-style guest rooms, where you find comfy beds and marble tubs. There's also a massage room, a sauna and fitness center as well as the resident bar, 1886. If you feel like venturing out with your pup, check out the hiking/biking trail six blocks from the hotel. Dog biscuits are on the room service menu in case you forget to pack treats. $50 fee. 25-pound weight limit.

Four Seasons Hotel: Austin
(512) 478-4500
98 San Jacinto Blvd (@ E Ceasar Chavez St)
Austin, Texas 78701
www.fourseasons.com/austin
Price Range: $$$$$

Only a short distance from the convention center and Austin's 6th Street, the luxurious Four Seasons Austin transports you to a world of lakeside tranquility. Their heated pool, tennis courts and golf course provide the perfect setting for a relaxing work-out. If you're seeking rejuvenation, check out the Four Season's sublime spa. Your pup can look forward to freshly baked dog biscuits, his own Four Seasons bowls, complimentary daily walks on the nearby hiking and biking trails and a dog room-service menu that includes German Shepard pie. Pets may not stay in the room unattended. No fee. 30-pound weight limit.

(214) - Dallas

Hotel Crescent Court
(214) 871-3200
400 Crescent Ct (between Maple Ave & Cedar Springs Rd)
Dallas, Texas 75201
www.crescentcourt.com
Price Range: $$$$$
A sister hotel to the Mansion on Turtle Creek, the Crescent Court offers European elegance in a culturally rich area. The hotel offers outstanding restaurants, and in addition to being on all of the appropriate best-hotel lists, the Crescent Court has received numerous accolades for its day spa. Across the courtyard you'll discover the world-class Shops and Galleries at the Crescent. The accommodating staff will walk your dog up to four times a day. Nearby services include a pet boutique and a vet, located around the corner. The neighborhood makes for scenic dog walking, and a small off-leash park is less than a mile away. $100 fee. 50-pound weight limit.

Mansion on Turtle Creek
(214) 559-2100
2821 Turtle Creek Blvd (@ Gillespie St)
Dallas, Texas 75219
www.mansiononturtlecreek.com
Price Range: $$$$$
Considered the best hotel in Dallas, the Mansion is the first American hotel to win *Travel & Leisure's* 2003 World's Best Service Award. Everything is absolutely exquisite in this five-star hotel located in beautiful Highland Park. The Mansion offers every amenity and service you can imagine. The always-accommodating staff will honor dog-walking requests. Water,

food bowls and treats are standard, and the staff will fetch missing essentials. Nearby parks and jogging trails offer picturesque on-leash walks, and the hotel is not too far from an off-leash dog park. $100 fee. 50-pound weight limit.

The Westin: City Center Dallas

(214) 979-9000
650 N Pearl St (between San Jacinto & Bryan sts)
Dallas, Texas 75201
www.starwood.com/westin/citycenterdallas

Price Range: $$$

If you give the Westin City Center advance warning, your dog gets bowls, treats, a bed, a leash and a collar. Your pup also has walking privileges throughout most of this enormous hotel, including the walkways around the 15-story atrium that lead to shops, restaurants and an indoor ice-skating rink. A mini-park also waits across the street. If you and your pup prefer a longer trek, go five blocks to the dog-friendly West End—which offers tree-lined streets and brick sidewalks. No fee. 40-pound weight limit.

(972) - Dallas, Frisco & Irving

Four Seasons Resort and Club: Dallas - Las Colinas

(972) 717-0700
4150 N MacArthur Blvd (off Byron Nelson Way)
Irving, Texas 75038
www.fourseasons.com/dallas

Price Range: $$$$$

A golfer's paradise, the Four Seasons Resort and Club in Dallas boasts a TPC championship course in Las Colinas, an elegant location that even non-golfers will love. Dogs will enjoy complimentary treats and their own Four Seasons bowls. However, keep in mind the Four Seasons Dallas does not allow pets to stay in the room unattended, so be prepared to pay a $15 service fee for a pet-sitter, plus $15 per hour with a three hour minimum. While a walking service is not provided, the hotel staff will walk dogs upon request. No fee. 15-pound weight limit.

The Westin: Galleria Dallas

(972) 934-9494
13340 Dallas Pkwy (@ LBJ Expressway)
Dallas, Texas 75240
www.starwood.com/westin/dallas
Price Range: $$$

The Galleria Mall is home to an indoor ice-skating rink, Saks, Tiffany's plus 200 other shops and restaurants, as well as the Westin Hotel. The tasteful decor is definitely high-end shopping-mall chic, with the Westin's signature Heavenly Bed the focal point of the guest rooms. Though dogs aren't allowed inside the mall, they can walk the hotel grounds and lobby (on leash). There are also plenty of grassy walking areas just north of the Westin. And the hotel offers dog amenities galore: a Westin Heavenly Dog Bed, food and water bowls, a placemat, treats, a list of dog-related services available through the concierge and bags for cleanup duties. No fee. 40-pound weight limit.

The Westin: Park Central

(972) 385-3000
12720 Merit Dr (between Highway 635 & Coit Rd)
Dallas, Texas 75251
www.starwood.com/westin/parkcentral
Price Range: $$$

Situated at the gateway to the Dallas Telecom Corridor, the Westin Park Central offers your pet the Love That Dog program with pet perks including a dog bed, bowls and treats, plus concierge-coordinated dog walking and pet-sitting. But you may want do the walking yourself at the nearby White Rock Lake Park, which contain plenty of room to run, roam and socialize. Beware: The local animal control does regular pet-tag checks. For a closer dog walk, the Westin offers a dog-friendly jogging trail behind the hotel. No fee. 40-pound weight limit.

The Westin: Stonebriar Resort
(972) 668-8000
1549 Legacy Dr (@ Highway 121)
Frisco, Texas 75034
www.starwood.com/westin/stonebriar
Price Range: $$$$
This magnificent Westin Resort, located in Frisco (a North Dallas suburb), is a golfer's paradise. Before playing a round on their Tom Fazio championship course, you can practice on their putting green and driving range. The Westin even offers lessons. Other offerings include the 200-foot lagoon-style pool complete with a water slide, hot tub and Aquabar. The hotel restaurant, Ernie's Legacy Grill, serves Southwestern cuisine. Shoppers have two choices: Willow Bend or the Stonebriar Center. Although there are no parks nearby, you can take your dog for a leashed walk on the field near the course: Just have your scooper handy. $100 deposit. 40-pound weight limit.

(817) – Fort Worth

The Ashton
(817) 332-0100
610 Main St (between 5th & 6th sts)
Fort Worth, Texas 76102
www.slh.com/ashton/
Price Range: $$$$$
A member of the prestigious Small Luxury Hotels of the World, the Ashton, which was built in 1915 and totally reno-

vated in 2001, is listed on the National Register of Historic
Places. Everything is exquisite in this smoke-free hotel, from
the wine cellar and bathtubs, to the Molton Brown toiletries
and the furnishings and bedding. The hotel restaurant, the Cafe
Ashton, is a special-occasion destination in its own right. Dogs
are welcome here, and the hotel owner will also provide you
with a list of his pet-care providers. If you feel like taking your
dog for a stroll, the Trinity River is just six blocks away. $150
deposit. 35-pound weight limit.

(713) - Houston

Four Seasons Hotel: Houston
(713) 650-1300
1300 Lamar St (@ Caroline St)
Houston, Texas 77010
www.fourseasons.com/houston
Price Range: $$$$$
From its blissful spa and pool to the Italian restaurant, Quattro,
the Four Seasons offers guests an oasis in the heart of
Houston's business and theater districts. Within this area, the
hotel offers complimentary town car service. You're also within
walking distance of many local attractions. Kid perks at this
family-friendly hotel include a welcome gift bag, milk and
cookies at bedtime, smaller robes, special toiletries and a children's menu. Dogs get complimentary walks by the staff and
their own Four Seasons bowls. Rather than leave your dog in
the room unattended, the hotel asks that you hire a pet-sitter
($12 an hour) or crate her. No fee. 15-pound weight limit.

The Lancaster Hotel
(713) 228-9500
701 Texas Ave (@ Louisiana Ave)
Houston, Texas 77002
www.slh.com/lancaster
Price Range: $$$$$

In a state where bigger usually means better, it is a testament to the quality of this boutique hotel—a member of the Small Leading Hotels of the World—that it is so revered by both visitors and locals. Built during the Roaring '20s, the Lancaster is located in the heart of the Houston business, theatre and restaurant district. While you're taking in a play and dinner, your small pup can stay cozy in your luxury suite. The concierge will locate sitting, walking or grooming services. $75 cleaning fee. 10-pound weight limit.

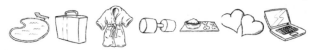

St. Regis: Houston
(713) 840-7600
1919 Briar Oaks Ln (@ San Felipe St)
Houston, Texas 77027
www.starwood.com/stregis/houston
Price Range: $$$$$

A *Travel & Leisure* 500 Best Hotels in the World pick, the elegantly grand St. Regis is located in the high-end neighborhood, River Oaks. This hotel offers plush accommodations, a blissful spa and world-class dining as well as a divine Tea Lounge. You're a short drive from the business and theater district, where the Galleria as well as Houston's sports and entertainment arenas are located. The St. Regis will take excellent care of your dog—beds, bowls and gourmet treats are regular hotel fare. And the dog-knowledgeable concierge will arrange walks and dog-care services. A dog park is close by. No fee. No weight limit.

The Westin: Galleria Houston
(713) 960-8100
5060 W Alabama St
(between McCue & S Post Oak rds)
Houston, Texas 77056
www.starwood.com/westin/galleria
Price Range: $$$

The Westin Galleria shares the honor of being Houston's premiere business hotel with its sister hotel—the Westin Oaks, located on the same block. The ambiance, corporate board-room with Southwestern accents, makes for tasteful, spacious rooms. You'll find ergonomic chairs and the signature Heavenly Bed in each suite, as well as high-speed Internet. The Daily Grill offers American cuisine, but you can also try Zucchini's and Shuckers at the Westin Oaks. Pet amenities include a Heavenly Dog Bed, bowls, a placemat, a collar and baggies. A dog-friendly park is across the street, plus plenty of other nearby walking areas. No fee. 40-pound weight limit.

The Westin: Oaks

(713) 960-8100
5011 Westheimer Rd
(@ S Post Oak Rd)
Houston, Texas 77056
www.starwood.com/westin/oaks

Price Range: $$$

Part of the Westin Houston duo, the Westin Oaks overlooks uptown Houston. It's located close to two convention centers, several museums, and connected to the Galleria Shopping Center. This business-oriented hotel offers high-speed Internet, the signature Heavenly Bed, an outdoor heated pool and numerous ballrooms and boardrooms. If you request a WestinWORKOUT room, you'll get a room with stationary bicycle and exercise balls. The hotel's Zucchini's Farm-To-Market offers local fare. There's also Shucker's Sports Bar, which is known for great seafood. Your dog gets a bed, bowls, treats and a welcome kit. A small lakeside park is within walking distance. No fee. 40-pound weight limit.

(281) – Houston

Sofitel: Houston

(281) 445-9000
425 N Sam Houston Pkwy East
(@ Beltway 8 West)
Houston, Texas 77060
www.sofitel.com

Price Range: $$$

Conveniently located in the heart of the North Houston business district, this Sofitel caters to the business professional. Complete with high-speed Internet and 15 reception halls, it's more likely than not that a conference will be going on during your stay. If you can steal away from the nametags and seminars, there's a tropical pool to lounge in, a fitness center and a nearby golf course. An excellent French-American restaurant, plus a fabulous bakery and a piano lounge are in the hotel. Your pup is free to roam the grassy grounds of the hotel, but be sure to crate him while unattended in the room. $50 fee. $200 deposit. No weight limit.

(210) – San Antonio

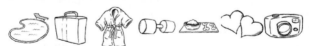

La Mansion del Rio

(800) 292-7300
112 College St
(@ N St. Mary's St)
San Antonio, Texas 78205
www.lamansion.com

Price Range: $$$$$

One of *Travel & Leisure's* 500 Greatest Hotels and named a favorite place by *Departures* magazine readers, this Spanish Colonial-style hotel—originally built over a century ago as a schoolhouse—is regarded as a historical treasure by the Texas Historical Commission. From the beautiful Spanish courtyards to the magnificent suites, everything is exquisite. La Mansion's restaurant, Las Canarias, receives raves. The San Antonio River Walk is just outside your balcony, and the Alamo is a few blocks away. The hotel requests that you not leave the dog in the room alone, so plan to take your pup with you or get a pet-sitter. Small pets only. $25 daily fee.

The Westin Riverwalk
(210) 224-6500
420 W Market St
(between S St. Mary's & Navarro sts)
San Antonio, Texas 78205
www.starwood.com/westin/riverwalk
Price Range: $$$

This luxe southern mansion, which Landed a spot on the 2003 *Condé Nast* Gold List, is right on San Antonio's famed Riverwalk. You can lounge in the sauna, at the pool bar or people watch from the vantage point of the Spanish inspired Caliza Grille. El Cafeto, the in-house bakery, has delicious croissants and features Starbucks coffee. If you're the roller-coaster type, Six Flags is a short drive away, as is the San Antonio zoo and several golf courses. The Westin provides your pup with its signature Heavenly Dog Bed, treats, bowls and baggies for leashed walks around the property. No fee. 40-pound weight limit.

Utah

(801) – Salt Lake City

Hotel Monaco: Salt Lake City

Hotel Monaco: Salt Lake City

(800) 805-1801
15 W 200 St
(@ S Main St)
Salt Lake City, Utah 84101
www.monaco-saltlakecity.com
Price Range: $$$

Colors clash and patterns collide but the resulting decor is fabulously chic at this Kimpton boutique hotel. The hotel's restaurant, Bambara, landed *Salt Lake* magazine's Best Restaurant, Best New Restaurant and Best Brunch awards. Your dog will receive complimentary dog bowls, treats and a bed upon arrival. Check out Pioneer and Liberty parks: They're both dog friendly and within walking distance of the hotel. The Monaco requests that you not leave your dog alone in the room. However, the concierge will schedule a pet-sitter for you. If you're traveling without your dog, the Monaco will loan you a goldfish to keep you company during your stay. No fee. No weight limit.

Vermont

(802) - Stowe

Green Mountain Inn
Topnotch At Showe Resort and Spa

Green Mountain Inn
(800) 253-7302
18 S Main St
(off Route 108)
Stowe, Vermont 05672
www.greenmountaininn.com
Price Range: $$$$$
Originally built in 1833 as a private home, the newly renovated Green Mountain Inn maintains a classic New England-ele-
gance. Winter activities include snowshoeing, sleigh rides and
ice skating. Summer offerings include fly-fishing. The pool is
heated year-round. You and your dog will be relegated to a
standard room, instead of a suite or village townhouse, and
you are asked to use the rear entrance when your pet needs to
go out. The 120 acres of private off-site trails make it all worth-
while. $20 daily fee. 50-pound weight limit.

Topnotch At Stowe Resort and Spa

(802) 253-8585
4000 Mountain Rd
(@ Brookdale Ln)
Stowe, Vermont 05672
www.topnotch-resort.com

Price Range: $$$$$

At this 120-acre luxury resort and spa, you can hike, fish, golf, ski, ice skate or snowshoe. But the resort specialty is the year-round tennis academy-ranked fourth in the country by *Tennis* magazine. Dogs are free to run leash-free around the expansive property or you can try one of the many nearby hiking trails, including the paved Quiet Path, a bicycle-free jaunt specifically for people (and dogs) who need a little peace. If your pup over-does it, arrange for the Rover Retreat service from the hotel spa with in-room massage or visit the posh grooming and boarding facilities next door. No fee. No weight limit.

Virginia

(703) - Arlington

The Ritz-Carlton, Pentagon City

(804) - Irvington & Richmond

Jefferson Hotel
The Tides Inn

(434) - Keswick

Keswick Hall

(703) - Arlington

The Ritz-Carlton: Pentagon City
(703) 415-5000
1250 S Hayes St
(@ 15th St)
Arlington, Virginia 22202
www.ritzcarlton.com/hotels/pentagon_city
Price Range: $$$$
The Pentagon City Ritz has everything the business traveler
might need, including high-speed Internet, and it's just across
the river from D.C. Perks include an indoor pool, Swedish and
Shiatsu massage, a fitness center—complete with personal
trainers-and two nearby golf courses. For your pup the Ritz
offers a low-fat menu, and entrees include lean ground beef
with mixed veggies and mashed potatoes, as well as low-fat
chicken with steamed brown rice. Informal dog-walking services are available through the concierge. But with dog-friendly
parks all around, you may want to walk him yourself. No fee.
No weight limit.

(804) – Irvington, Richmond

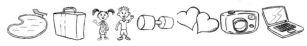

Jefferson Hotel

(800) 424-8014
101 West Franklin St
(@ Adams St)
Richmond, Virginia 23220
www.jefferson-hotel.com

Price Range: $$$$

Rumor has it the steps of *Gone With the Wind's* Tara were
inspired by the majestic steps of the Jefferson Hotel. Dating
back to 1895, this exquisite five-star hotel is one of the
Historic Hotels of America and Preferred Hotels and Resorts
Worldwide honoree. The classic decor, in keeping with the
history of the hotel, is inviting and comfortable. The Jefferson
boasts two restaurants: the formal Lemaire and the more casu-
al TJ's, and afternoon tea is served in the Palm Court Lobby.
The Jefferson offers a fitness center as well as an indoor pool
complete with skylights. The hotel will handle your dog-walking duties ($15 per hour). $35 daily fee. No weight limit.

The Tides Inn

(800) 843-3746
480 King Carter Dr
(off Rte 200)
Irvington, Virginia 22480
www.tidesinn.com

Price Range: $$$$$

Just off Chesapeake Bay, the Tides Inn sits on a bluff overlooking Carter's Creek on the Rappahannock River. The Inn
features an abundance of water activities, including yacht
cruises, fishing, canoeing and sailing lessons. Those who prefer
dry land can relax at the spa or play a round of golf at the
Golden Eagle Golf Club. History buffs may want to make the
hour drive to the birthplaces of General Lee and George
Washington, the Mary Ball Washington Museum and Colonial

Williamsburg. All of the nearby hiking trails, gardens and beaches allow dogs to roam off leash. The staff leaves treats at turndown. $35 fee. No weight limit.

(434) - Keswick

Keswick Hall

(800) 274-5391
701 Club Dr
(@ Fairway Dr)
Keswick, Virginia 22947
www.keswick.com
Price Range: $$$$$

Suffice it to say that this exquisite Orient Express hotel is a regular fixture on all of the noteworthy best-hotel lists. Set in Virginia hunt country, Keswick Hall offers stunning views of the Blue Ridge Mountains. The decor is Southern Virginia-elegant and the service takes Southern hospitality to a new level. Pet-friendly rooms include private terraces and the hotel's Pampered Pooch service welcomes dogs with gourmet treats, comfy beds and a seasonal dog room-service menu. Except for the Arnold Palmer golf course, your leashed dog is welcome anywhere on the property. Sitting is available for $8 an hour. $75 nightly fee, plus a $50 cleaning charge. 75-pound weight limit.

Washington

(206) - Seattle

The Alexis Hotel
Hotel Monaco: Seattle
Hotel Vintage Park
Sorrento
W: Seattle
The Westin: Seattle

(360) - Blaine

Semiahmoo Resort

(206) - Seattle

The Alexis Hotel
(866) 356-8894
1007 1st Ave (@ Madison St)
Seattle, Washington 98104
www.alexishotel.com
Price Range: $$$$$
This charming four-star boutique hotel, decorated exclusively with the work of artists from the Pacific Northwest, welcomes all guests from dignitaries to dogs. Rooms range from a comfortable standard, to signature John Lennon, Miles Davis, honeymoon, spa or fireplace suites. Guest perks include a complimentary evening wine reception and an on-site Aveda Spa. Your pup will receive a complimentary dog bed, treats and water bowl, complete with bottled water upon arrival. The hotel will arrange for pet-sitting, unless of course you want to splurge on a private grooming, dog massage or acupuncture session, which the hotel will also book for you. No fee. No weight limit.

Hotel Monaco: Seattle

(800) 715-6513
1101 4th Ave (@ Spring St)
Seattle, Washington 98101
www.monaco-seattle.com

Price Range: $$$

The decor at the plush Monaco Hotels takes on a life all its own. Eclectic perks include twice-a-week chair massage, fortune telling, and of course, the Kimpton hotel's standard complimentary evening wine hour. If you're traveling without your dog, the hotel will loan you a goldfish to keep you company during your stay. The Monaco has raincoats on hand for all dog guests, and will donate $5 to the King County Humane Society if you purchase one to take home. Your pup will also get a treat on his dog bed each evening. Pet-sitting is easily arranged through the concierge at this boutique Kimpton hotel. No fee. No weight limit.

Hotel Vintage Park

(800) 853-3914
1100 5th Ave (@ Spring St)
Seattle, Washington 98101
www.hotelvintagepark.com

Price Range: $$$$$

Listed on the national register of historic places, the Hotel Vintage Park is a regular on both the *Condé Nast Traveler* Gold List and *Travel & Leisure's* Top 500 Hotels in the World list. This vineyard-inspired hotel brings the Northwest wine country to Seattle, making the complimentary wine hour—a Kimpton Hotel standard—particularly special. One look at the lavish decor in your guest room and you may think you've fallen into the genie bottle from *I Dream of Jeannie*. With the hotel's Pets Love the Park program, dogs receive Vintage Park dog tags as well as grape-shaped treats. The concierge will also make any pet-care arrangements you may need. No fee. No weight limit.

Sorrento

(800) 426-1265
900 Madison St
(@ 9th St)
Seattle, Washington 98104
www.hotelsorrento.com

Price Range: $$$$$

This boutique luxury hotel in the heart of downtown Seattle allows dogs at no extra charge, but their catering services and amenities are for business travelers and shoppers. People perks include fine dining, sumptuous linens and a Nordstrom's on the first floor, but dogs must be content with on-leash neighborhood walks or a leashed romp around Volunteer Park a mile and a half away. There's not much nearby in the way of dog services or supplies, so bring a kennel for your room and a well-stocked travel bag for your pup. No fee. No weight limit.

W: Seattle

(206) 264-6000
1112 4th Ave (@ Spring St)
Seattle, Washington 98101
www.starwood.com/whotels/seattle

Price Range: $$$

The W, with its heavenly fireplace and exceedingly comfortable and chic decor, is as hip a sanctuary as you will find in downtown Seattle. It was picked for both the *Travel & Leisure* 100 Best Hotels list and the *Condé Nast Traveler* Gold List. The W's standard package includes a toy, a treat, a tag and clean-up bags. In-room dog necessities include a bed, food and water bowls, a Pet in Room sign and turn-down treat. Room service will deliver items you forgot, from leashes and toys to food and treats. $25 a night, plus a $100 cleaning fee. 80-pound weight limit.

The Westin: Seattle

(206) 728-1000
1900 5th Ave (@ Stewart St)
Seattle, Washington 98101
www.starwood.com/westin/seattle

Price Range: $$$

Close to shopping, museums, a convention center and Safeco Field, the Westin Seattle is not only conveniently located, it boasts plenty of amenities, including the Westin's signature Heavenly Bed (and a smaller version for your pup), a 24-hour fitness center, an indoor heated pool and gorgeous city views. Seattle might just be the most dog-friendly place around—pups under 20 pounds can ride the monorail, and leashed dogs are allowed in the Seattle Center, the site of the 1962 World's Fair. Pups are even welcome at nearby Pike Place Market, which offers nine acres of fresh seafood—be sure to keep your pup on a tight leash! No fee. 50-pound weight limit.

(360) - Blaine

Semiahmoo Resort

(800) 278-7488
9565 Semiahmoo Pkwy
(near Drayton Harbor)
Blaine, Washington 98230
www.semiahmoo.com

Price Range: $$$$$

This seaside resort offers plenty of activities for the whole family: sailing, kayaking, tennis, hiking, rollerblading, salmon fishing, horseback riding and skiing in the winter. Other offerings include Washington's top two golf courses, a heated pool, a sauna and an indoor running track. The hotel also boasts a full-service spa. Dining options include the more formal Stars, as well as the Packer Lounge and Oyster Bar: Both overlook Semiahmoo Bay. The Gift Shop Cafe and Coffee Bar also offers snacks and sandwiches. Rooms include a fireplace and high-speed Internet access. You can daytrip up to dog-friendly Seattle or Vancouver a few hours away. $50 fee. 40-pound weight limit.

Wyoming

(307) - Teton Village

Four Seasons Resort: Jackson Hole

Four Seasons Resort: Jackson Hole
(307) 732-5000
7680 Granite Loop Rd
(off Teton Village Rd)
Teton Village, Wyoming 83025
www.fourseasons.com/jacksonhole
Price Range: $$$$$
The luxe Four Seasons Jackson Hole takes the mountain lodge
to new heights. The breathtaking Teton mountains are close by
and perfect for outdoor activities: skiing, fly-fishing, golf,
horseback riding, mountain biking, tennis, rafting as well as
plenty of hiking with your pup. The pool is heated year-round,
with heated towels, s'mores and hot chocolate offered during
the winter. Your dog will also enjoy treats upon arrival, his
own food and water bowls filled with Evian water and a Four
Seasons dog bed. The hotel does not formally offer dog walking, but the bellman will walk dogs upon request. The
concierge will make pet-sitting arrangements for you. No fee.
15-pound weight limit.

In a Pinch...

If you and your dog need a place to stay in a pinch, the following is a list of national hotel chains that accept pets.

Motel 6
(800) 4-Motel6
www.motel6.com
Price Range: $
Inexpensive is the operative word for Motel 6. With over 350 locations you're bound to come across one in your travels. Each location comes with free HBO and ESPN and free morning coffee. Other than that you'll get the basics—a bed to sleep in and a sink to wash your face in. For the budget conscience, or those that get stuck on the road, it's a decent option. Their dog policy is pretty lenient: one well-behaved pet per room.

Red Roof Inn
(800) 733-7663
www.redroof.com
Price Range: $
Despite the college dorm aesthetic, the Red Roof Inn is a palatable option due to its 330 interstate-convenient locations, mostly in the Midwest, the South and the East, and inexpensive rates. At $45 a night, it's definitely a bargain. Amenities include HBO, ESPN and a clock radio. Their pet policy allows one well-behaved pet per room, and you must declare your pet at check-in. The hotel does not allow pets to be left alone in the room.

Residence Inn
(800) 331-3131
www.residenceinn.com
Price Range: $
Designed for interim stays between houses or for working on location, the Marriott's Residence Inn is a nice option for those wanting a few more amenities than a bed and bath. Complimentary offerings include a hot breakfast, a *USA Today*, high-speed Internet access and an all-purpose Sport Court. Major Perk: If you leave a grocery list at the front desk, someone will shop for you and leave your groceries in your suite. You can mingle at the weekly barbeques or the nightly social hours. The longer you stay, the better your rate is. No weight limit. Fees vary.

Studio 6

(888) 897-0202
www.staystudio6.com
Price Range: $
The extended-stay version of Motel 6, Studio 6 offers low rates
for rooms with kitchens. Offerings include free HBO and CNN,
guest laundry and late check-in. Rooms—best described as
retirement home-chic—come with a refrigerator, microwave,
stove top, coffee maker, dishes, cooking utensils and a dining
table. The pet policy allows for one well-behaved pet per room.
$10 per day fee, with a maximum of $50. No weight limit.

TownePlace Suites

(800) 257-3000
www.towneplacesuites.com
Price Range: $
The Marriott-owned TownePlace Suites offers extended-stay
accommodations. The sterile decor leans towards Ikea and
comes complete with a bed, desk, couch and tables. Hotel
amenities include an exercise room, swimming pool, a bar-
beque area and guest laundry. Rooms also have refrigerators,
ovens, utensils and HBO. Some branches charge a deposit or
cleaning fee. No weight limit.

Preparing & Packing For Your Trip

ESSENTIALS

- Kennel or crate that your pup can stand, sit, lie down and turn around in.
- Bottled water
- Baggies
- Leash
- Collar:
    - ID tag with phone number (If your dog requires daily medication, it is good to note it on the tag)
    - Current license and rabies vaccination
- Medication (If necessary)
- A copy of your dog's vaccination records
- Enough food for your trip, plus a reserve supply
- Can opener and spoon if you feed your pup wet food
- Brush
- Treats
- Carpet cleaner
- Paper towels
- First Aid Kit:
    - Bandages & Tape
    - Gauze
    - Hydrogen peroxide
    - Local emergency numbers
    - Matches
    - Muzzle
    - Ointment
    - Rubbing alcohol
    - Scissors
    - Thermometer
    - Tweezers

SUNSHINE ESSENTIALS

- Sunscreen—SPF 30 on:
    - Pads of your dog's feet
    - Any exposed or partially exposed skin: ears, stomach, nose etc.
    - Dogs with a white or thin coat
- Bottled water
- A spray bottle to spritz your dog
- Extra towels for sandy or wet pups
- Dog shampoo
- Handkerchief (to wet for cooling down your pup)
- Signs of Heatstroke:
    - Rapid panting
    - Wide eyes
    - Salivating
    - Staggering
    - Weakness
    - Temperature above 105 degrees

SNOWY & COLD WEATHER

- Booties if your pup will be in the snow or ice, or if your pup will be exposed to salted sidewalks or roads.
    - Note: Do NOT let your pup lick his paws after walking on a salted road. The salt is poisonous.
- A waterproof jacket for your pup
- Extra blankets
- Space blanket for warming up cold pups
- Extra towels for wet pups
- Thick socks (children sized) to fit your pup
- Signs of Hypothermia:
    - Violent shivering
    - Listlessness
    - Weak pulse
    - Lethargy
    - Temperature under 95 degrees

ROAD TRIP ESSENTIALS

- A crate or canine seatbelt
- Motion-sickness pills or sedatives (if necessary)
- Leash
- Water with bowl
- Baggies
- Paper towels
- Handi-wipes

Note: Do NOT leave your dog in the car unattended. In hot (and even warm) climates dogs suffocate very quickly when left in an enclosed vehicle. Also, it only takes a moment for someone to steal your dog.

Airline Rules
within the continental United States

Airlines require a health certificate issued no more than 10 days prior to your dog's departure. Your pet must be issued a clean bill of health by a veterinarian and be current on all of his vaccinations. If your return flight is outside the 10-day period, some airlines will require another health certificate, while other airlines are more flexible. Always be sure to review their policies before making final arrangements.

Pets must be eight weeks old and weaned before traveling. Most airlines allow two carry-on pets per coach passenger, and one pet per first-class passenger.

TRANQUILIZERS

Sedating your pet is discouraged the by American Veterinary Medical Association and most airlines. Drugs can be unpredictable at high altitudes. If your vet decides tranquilizers are necessary, you must list on your dog's kennel the type of medication, dosage plus how and when the drug was administered.

PETS AS CARGO

The kennel...
- Must be sturdy, leak-proof and include a hinged or sliding door.
- Kennels must have grips or handles for lifting. While the kennel must be ventilated, no part of your dog's body should be able to fit through the kennel openings.
- Two empty dishes for food and water should be accessible from the outside.
- Don't lock the kennel door.
- If the kennel has wheels, they must have a locking device.

Your dog... must be able to stand and sit upright without his head touching the top of the kennel as well as turn around and lie down comfortably.

You need to...
- Make sure your pet's nails get clipped prior to your trip to prevent them from hooking onto the kennel.

- Place absorbent bedding—such as towels, blankets or news paper—inside the kennel. Note: Do NOT use colored newspaper. The ink may be toxic to your pet.
- Label the kennel with your pet's name, your contact information and your dog's final destination.
- Attach feeding instructions over a 24-hour period to the kennel.
- Display a Live Animals label with letters at least one-inch high on the top and on at least one side of the kennel.
- Label the kennel This End Up on at least two sides.
- Offer your pet food and water within four hours of check-in: Airport officials will have you confirm this with a signature.
- Reconfirm your pet's reservation 24 to 48 hours before departure to verify that temperatures are within acceptable ranges for your dog to fly.

OTHER HELPFUL HINTS

- Book a direct, nonstop flight.
- Avoid holiday or weekend travel.
- Carry a current photograph of your pet.

AIRLINE PET POLICIES

- **Note:** All weight limits include the combined weight of the dog and carrier/kennel.

American Airlines
(800) 433-7300
www.americanairlines.com
In-Cabin Pet:
Price: $80 each way
Carrier size limit: 23 in x 20 in x 9 in
Weight limit: 20 pounds
Pet as Cargo:
Price: $100 each way
Kennel size limit: 40 in x 20 in x 30 in
Weight limit: 100 pounds
Temperature restrictions: The outside temperature during the trip must be between 45 degrees and 85 degrees, 75 degrees for cats and pug-nosed dogs.

Continental

(800) 523-3273
Animal Desk: (800) 575-3335
www.continental.com
In-Cabin Pet:
Price: $80 each way
Weight limit: 10 pounds
Carrier size limit: 22 in x 14 in x 9 in
Pet as Cargo:
Price: $99 to $329 each way
Weight limit: 150 pounds
Kennel size limit: 40 in x 27 in x 30 in
Temperature restrictions: None
• Each dollar spent on pet travel is equivalent to a mile on the One Pass rewards program.

Delta

(800) 221-1212
www.delta.com
In-Cabin Pet:
Price: $75 each way
Weight limit: None
Carrier size limit: 17 in x 12 in x 8 in
Pet as Cargo:
Weight limit: 51 pounds
Price: $75 each way
Kennel size limit: 48 in x 32 in x 35 in
Temperature restrictions: The outside temperature during the trip must be between 45 degrees to 85 degrees, 75 degrees for cats and pug-nosed dogs.
Blackout days: May 15 – Sept. 15

Jet Blue

(800) 538-2583
www.jetblue.com
In-Cabin Pet:
Price: $50 each way
Weight limit: 20 pounds
Carrier size limit: 18 in x 15 in x 8 in
Pet as Cargo:
Jet Blue does not accept pets as cargo.

Northwest Airlines

(800) 225-2525
Pet Center Information Line: (888) 692-4738
www.nwa.com
In-Cabin Pet:
Price: $80 fee each way
Weight limit: 15-pounds
Carrier size limit: 17 in x 12.3 in x 8 in
Pet as Cargo:
Weight limit: 25 pounds to 150 pounds
Price: $139 to $299
Kennel size limit: 40 in x 27 in x 30 in
Temperature restrictions: The outside temperature during the trip must be between 45 degrees and 85 degrees, 75 degrees for cats and pug-nosed dogs.
Blackout days: June 1 – Sept. 15

Southwest Airlines

Only service animals permitted to fly.

U.S. Airways

(800) 943-5436
www.usairways.com
In-Cabin Pet:
Price $100 each way
Carrier size limit: 21 in x 16 in x 8 in
Pet as Cargo:
Price: $100 each way
Weight limit: 100 pounds
Kennel size limit: 48 in x 32 in x 35 in
Temperature restrictions: The outside temperature during the trip must be between 45 degrees and 85 degrees, 75 degrees for cats and pug-nosed dogs
• U.S. Airways does not make reservations for pets as cargo.
   They operate on a first-come/first-served basis.

United

(800) 864-8331
www.united.com
In-Cabin Pet:
Price: $80 each way
Weight limit: 20 pounds
Carrier size limit: 17 in x 12 in x 8 in

Pet as Cargo:
Price: $100 to $200
Weight limit: 150 pounds
Kennel size limit: 40 in x 27 in x 30 in
Temperature restrictions: The outside temperature during the
trip must be between 45 degrees and 85 degrees, 75 degrees for
cats and pug-nosed dogs.

Car Rental Agencies

Most car rental agencies allow pets with no additional fee or
weight limit, but you will be charged for any damage your dog
does to the vehicle. To avoid a cleaning fee, make sure to clean
up any pet hair before returning the car.

Avis
(800) 331-1212
www.avis.com
No fee. No weight limit.

Budget
(800) 527-0700
www.buget.com
No fee. No weight limit.

Dollar
Does not allow pets.

Enterprise
(800) 261-7331
www.enterprise.com
No fee. No weight limit.

Hertz
(800) 654-3131
www.hertz.com
No fee. No weight limit.

Index

5

5th Avenue Suites **152**

7

70 Park Avenue Hotel **132**

A

Alexis Hotel, The **180**
American Airlines **192**
Argonaut Hotel **15**
Ashton, The **168**
Avalon Beverly Hills **33**
Avis Car Rental **195**

B

Barnsley Gardens Resort **87**
Beverly Hills Hotel & Bungalows **33**
Beverly Hilton **34**
Brazilian Court **80**
Brown Palace Hotel **55**
Budget Car Rental **195**

C

Calistoga Ranch **24**
Carlyle, The **126**
Chambers Hotel **133**
Charles Hotel **104**
Charleston Place **161**
Chateau Marmont **42**
Chesterfield Hotel **80**
Colombia Gorge Hotel, The **184**
Columbia Gorge Hotel **152**

Continental Airlines **193**
Cypress Hotel **29**

D

Delamar Greenwich Harbor **58**
Delta Airlines **193**
Dollar Car Rental **195**
Drake, The **133**
Driskill, The **164**

E

Eden Roc Resort and Spa **73**
Eliot Hotel, The **105**
Elk Mountain Resort **52**
Enterprise Car Rental **195**

F

Fifteen Beacon **105**
Four Points Sheraton **11**
Four Seasons Hotel: Atlanta **84**
Four Seasons Hotel: Austin **164**
Four Seasons Hotel: Aviara, North San Diego **47**
Four Seasons Hotel: Boston **106**
Four Seasons Hotel: Chicago **90**
Four Seasons Hotel: Houston **169**
Four Seasons Hotel: Las Vegas **120**
Four Seasons Hotel: Los Angeles - Beverly Hills **34**
Four Seasons Hotel: Miami **74**
Four Seasons Hotel: New York **134**
Four Seasons Hotel: Newport Beach **44**
Four Seasons Hotel: Philadelphia **155**
Four Seasons Hotel: San Francisco **15**
Four Seasons Hotel: Washington, D.C. **61**
Four Seasons Resort and Club: Dallas - Las Colinas **166**
Four Seasons Resort: Jackson Hole **185**
Four Seasons Resort: Palm Beach **81**
Four Seasons Resort: Santa Barbara **50**
Four Seasons Resort: Scottsdale - Troon North **10**

G

Galleria Park Hotel **16**
Glendorn **158**
Green Mountain Inn **175**
Green Valley Ranch Resort and Spa **121**
Greenporter Hotel and Spa **142**

H

Harbor Court Hotel **16**
Hawthorne Hotel, The **111**
Hay-Adams Hotel **62**
Heathman Hotel, The **153**
Hertz Car Rental **195**
Hotel 71 **91**
Hotel Allegro **91**
Hotel Bel Air **35**
Hotel Commonwealth **107**
Hotel Cosmo **44**
Hotel Crescent Court **165**
Hotel DuPont **60**
Hotel George, The **62**
Hotel Healdsburg **25**
Hotel Helix **63**
Hotel Jerome **53**
Hotel Madera **63**
Hotel Marlowe **107**
Hotel Monaco: Chicago **92**
Hotel Monaco: Denver **56**
Hotel Monaco: New Orleans **98**
Hotel Monaco: Salt Lake City **174**
Hotel Monaco: San Francisco **17**
Hotel Monaco: Seattle **181**
Hotel Monaco: Washington, D.C. **64**
Hotel Palomar **17**
Hotel Rouge **64**
Hotel Teatro **56**
Hotel Telluride **53**
Hotel Triton **18**
Hotel Vintage Park **181**
Hotel Vintage Plaza **153**

I

Iberville Suites, The **99**
Inn at Perry Cabin, The **103**
Inn at Rancho Santa Fe, The **49**
Inn by the Sea **102**

J

James Hotels Scottsdale **11**
Jefferson Hotel **178**
Jefferson Hotel D.C. **65**
Jet Blue **65**

K

Keswick Hall **179**

L

L'Ermitage Beverly Hills **33**
La Mansion del Rio **172**
La Quinta Resort & Club **46**
La Valencia **48**
Lake Placid Lodge **143**
Lancaster Hotel, The **169**
Langham Hotel **108**
Le Meridien: Beverly Hills **36**
Le Meridien: Minneapolis **116**
Le Merigot Marriott **36**
Le Parker Meridian **134**
Lodge at Vail, The **54**
Loews, The: Hard Rock Hotel **78**
Lowell, The **126**

M

Madison D.C., The **65**
Mandarin Oriental: D.C. **66**
Mandarin Oriental: Miami **74**
Mandarin Oriental: New York **130**
Mandarin Oriental: San Francisco **18**
Mansion on Turtle Creek **165**
Maple Tree Inn **29**

Maritime Hotel **140**
Marquette, The **117**
Marriott **11**
Mayfair House Hotel **75**
Monticello Inn **19**
Motel 6 **186**
Muse, The **135**

N

Nine Zero Hotel **134**
Nine Zero Hotel, The **108**
Northwest Airlines **194**
Novotel **15**

O

Onyx Hotel **109**

P

Palace Hotel **20**
Paramount Hotel **135**
Peninsula, The: Beverly Hills **37**
Peninsula, The: New York **127**
Phillips Club **164**
Phillips Club, The **130**
Phoenician, The **11**
Pierre, The **127**
Plaza Athenee, The **128**
Point, The: Saranac Lake **143**
Prescott Hotel, The **20**

R

Red Roof Inn **186**
Regency, The **128**
Regent, The: Beverly Wilshire **37**
Residence Inn **186**
RIHGA Royal **136**
Rittenhouse Hotel **156**
Ritz-Carlton, The: Half Moon Bay **27**
Ritz-Carlton, The: Boston **109**
Ritz-Carlton, The: Boston Common **110**

Ritz-Carlton, The: Buckhead **85**
Ritz-Carlton, The: Chicago **92**
Ritz-Carlton, The: Cleveland **148**
Ritz-Carlton, The: Coconut Grove **75**
Ritz-Carlton, The: Dearborn **114**
Ritz-Carlton, The: Georgetown **66**
Ritz-Carlton, The: Huntington Hotel & Spa **43**
Ritz-Carlton, The: Lake Las Vegas **121**
Ritz-Carlton, The: Marina del Rey **38**
Ritz-Carlton, The: New York, Battery Park **140**
Ritz-Carlton, The: Palm Beach **96**
Ritz-Carlton, The: Pentagon City **177**
Ritz-Carlton, The: Philadelphia **156**
Ritz-Carlton, The: San Francisco **21**
Ritz Carlton, The: Sarasota **93**
Ritz-Carlton, The: South Beach **77**
Ritz-Carlton, The: St. Louis **118**
Ritz-Carlton, The: Washington, D.C. **67**
Ritz-Carlton, The: New Orleans **99**
Ritz-Carlton, The: New York, Central Park **131**
RiverPlace Hotel **154**

S

St. Regis Club at the Essex House **131**
St. Regis: Aspen **54**
St. Regis: Houston **170**
St. Regis: Los Angeles **38**
St. Regis: Monarch Beach **45**
St. Regis: Washington, D.C. **67**
Salishan Lodge & Golf Resort **151**
San Ysidro Ranch **51**
Seaport Hotel **110**
Semiahmoo Resort **183**
Serrano Hotel **21**
Sheraton **13**
Sherry-Netherland Hotel, The **129**
Shore Club **76**
Siena Hotel **145**
Sir Francis Drake, The **22**
Sky Hotel **55**
Sofitel: Chicago O'Hare **96**
Sofitel: Chicago Water Tower **93**
Sofitel: Houston **172**

Sofitel: Lafayette Square **68**
Sofitel: Los Angeles **39**
Sofitel: Miami **76**
Sofitel: Minneapolis **117**
Sofitel: New York **136**
Sofitel: Philadelphia **157**
Sofitel: San Francisco Bay **27**
SoHo Grand Hotel **141**
Sorrento **182**
Southwest Airlines **194**
Studio 6 **187**
Surrey, The **129**
Sutton Place Hotel **93**

T

Tabard Inn **68**
Talbott Hotel **94**
Ten Thousand Waves **124**
The Ritz-Carlton, Pentagon City **219**
Tides Hotel, The **77**
Tides Inn, The **178**
Topaz Hotel **69**
Topnotch at Stowe Resort and Spa **176**
TownPlace Suites **187**
Tuscan Inn at Fisherman's Wharf **22**

U

U.S. Airways **194**
United Airlines **194**

V

Viceroy Santa Monica **39**
Villa Florence **23**
Vintage Inn **25**

W

W: Atlanta **87**
W: Los Angeles **40**
W: New Orleans - French Quarter **100**
W: New Orleans- Riverwalk **100**
W: New York- Lexington **137**

W: New York- The Court **137**

W: New York- The Tuscany **138**

W: New York- Times Square **138**

W: New York- Union Square **139**

W: San Diego **49**

W: San Francisco **23**

W: Seattle **182**

W: Silicon Valley- Newark **26**

Walt Disney World Swan **79**

Westin Grand Bohemian Orlando **79**

Westin Resort, The: Hilton Head Island **162**

Westin Riverwalk, The **173**

Westin, The: Atlanta Airport **85**

Westin, The: Atlanta North at Perimeter **88**

Westin, The: Bonaventure Hotel & Suites **42**

Westin, The: Buckhead Atlanta **86**

Westin, The: Casuarina Hotel & Spa **122**

Westin, The: Century Plaza Hotel & Spa **41**

Westin, The: Charlotte **146**

Westin, The: Chicago River North **94**

Westin, The: Cincinnati **148**

Westin, The: City Center Dallas **166**

Westin, The: Columbus **147**

Westin, The: Convention Center Pittsburgh **158**

Westin, The: Copley Place **111**

Westin, The: Crown Center **119**

Westin, The: Detroit Metropolitan Airport **113**

Westin, The: Embassy Row **69**

Westin, The: Essex House on Central Park **132**

Westin, The: Fort Lauderdale **73**

Westin, The: Galleria Dallas **167**

Westin, The: Galleria Houston **170**

Westin, The: Grand **70**

Westin, The: Horton Plaza **50**

Westin, The: Indianapolis **97**

Westin, The: Innisbrook Golf Resort **82**

Westin, The: Kierland Resort & Spa **12**

Westin, The: La Paloma Resort & Spa **12**

Westin, The: Long Beach **44**

Westin, The: Los Angeles Airport **41**

Westin, The: Michigan Avenue Chicago **95**

Westin, The: Mission Hills Resort **47**

Westin, The: New York at Times Square **139**

Westin, The: O Hare **96**

Westin, The: Oaks **171**

Westin, The: Oklahoma City **150**

Westin, The: Palo Alto **28**

Westin, The: Park Central **167**

Westin, The: Pasadena **43**

Westin, The: Peachtree Plaza **86**

Westin, The: Philadelphia **157**

Westin, The: Portland **154**

Westin, The: Princeton at Forrestal Village **123**

Westin, The: Providence **160**

Westin, The: San Francisco Airport **28**

Westin, The: Santa Clara **30**

Westin, The: Savannah Harbor Golf Resort & Spa **88**

Westin, The: Seattle **183**

Westin, The: South Coast Plaza **46**

Westin, The: Southfield Detroit **114**

Westin, The: St. Francis **24**

Westin, The: St. Louis **119**

Westin, The: Stamford **58**

Westin, The: Stonebriar Resort **168**

Westin, The: Tabor Center **57**

Westin, The: Waltham-Boston **112**

Westin, The: Westminster **57**

Whitehall Hotel, The **95**

Wigwam Resort and Golf Club, The **13**

Willard InterContinental Washington **70**

Willcox, The **162**

Windsor Court Hotel **101**